Your Spiritual Geneti

M000084283

SOUL DNA

ULTIMATE EDITION

Jennifer O'Neill

First Print Edition: April 2012

Cover and interior by Streetlight Graphics.

Table of Contents

SOUL DNA

What is Soul DNA?   11

Your Creation Was Extensive   13

Understanding Universal Laws   23

Your Physical Body and Your Spiritual Health   37

The Gift of Free Will   45

Charting Your Life Path   51

Who Are Your Spirit Guides?   61

Career and Money Flow   73

The Pursuit of Happiness   81

What is Soul Chemistry?   93

Your Energetic Vibration   107

"The Law of Attraction" Simplified   117

Intuition & Psychic Ability   125

Consciousness Web   137

Past Lives and Past Life Memories   141

Releasing Your Physical Body   147

KEYS TO THE SPIRIT WORLD

What Is A Spirit Guide?   157

What Do Spirit Guides Look Like?   165

How Do Spirit Guides Communicate?   171

What Is It Like To Receive Communications From

Your Spirit Guide?   181

Chakras and Spirit Communication   187

10 Tips For Working With Spirit Guides and Spirits   197

Communicating With Spirit Guides Through Writing   213

Spirit Guide Communication Through Dreaming   217

Spirit Guide Communication Meditation   227

Five Common "Blocks"   233

PURSUIT OF HAPPINESS

Spiritual Rule #1

Understand You Are a Reflection of Your Choices   243

Spiritual Rule #2

Do Not Let Your Relationship Status Define Your Happiness 249

Spiritual Rule #3
Remove All Contingency Clauses You Have Attached To
Your Happiness   253

Spiritual Rule #4
Release Yourself From Expectations   257

Spiritual Rule #5
Do Not Hold Anyone Else Responsible For Your Happiness   261

Spiritual Rule #6
Pursue At Least One of Your Dreams   267

Spiritual Rule #7
Stop Looking For Happiness In the Future and Learn To
Experience Happiness In the Present   275

Spiritual Rule #8
Negative Thinking Is Contagious...So Protect Yourself
From Other People's Thinking   279

Spiritual Rule #9
Do Not Take Other People's Unhappiness Personally   285

Spiritual Rule #10
Implement Change   289

Spiritual Rule #11
Don't Let Fear Bully You   293

Spiritual Rule #12
Worry Less   297

Spiritual Rule #13
Let It Go...   301

Spiritual Rule #14
Stop Saving Your Happiness For Special Occasions   307

Spiritual Rule #15
Spend Some Time Creating Your Future   311

Spiritual Rule #16
Get Rid of Your Poverty Mindset!   317

Spiritual Rule #17
Love Unconditionally   323

Spiritual Rule #18
Take Care of Yourself Physically   329

Spiritual Rule #19
Listen To More Music   333

Spiritual Rule #20
Give and Appreciate   337

Spiritual Rule #21
Embrace the Power You Hold   341

Appendix 1   345

Appendix 2   347

Appendix 3   353

INSPIRATIONAL QUOTES

How To Use This Section of the Book: 361

Quotes   363

What is Soul DNA?

Soul DNA is your spiritual genetic system. Just as you have a physical genetic system, you also have a spiritual genetic system. We were all created from one. This is what is referred to in the Universal Laws as "The Law of One or Oneness." More commonly people refer to this as source, or energy, and in many instances, God. What this means is we are all a part of a larger one. As part of this larger one, every spiritual being is created with a spiritual genetic system. In this genetic system you are given all of the spiritual tools needed to achieve great success. The way in which you utilize these tools, however, is left up to each individual.

Your spiritual genetic system is made up of nine main components:

1) Gifts and Talents – Areas that you are gifted in or talented in, this defines your purpose.
2) Abilities – Your psychic abilities or spiritual GPS.
3) Free Will – Self will, the ability to make choices.
4) Spiritual Memory Bank – This memory bank contains all of the memories from each physical lifetime as well as spiritual memories and experiences that you have while in your natural state.
5) Reincarnation – The ability to take physical form, with the intention of learning and growing spiritually from each experience.
6) Communication System – The ability to communicate and stay connected at all times with other spirits, or the spirit world.
7) Energetic System – Everyone has an energy system and this system offers a vibration.
8) Universal Understanding or "Knowing" – As spiritual beings Universal Laws apply to us and thus, we must follow them.
9) Happiness – A gift of God.

You will learn about these things and more throughout this book, and hopefully you will be left with a greater understanding of how powerful you truly are! You were built to succeed, it is in your Soul DNA.

Your Creation Was Extensive

Every one of you is a gift of God, a special creation. Your uniqueness was intentional. You are all meant to be different from one another. Think of yourselves like snowflakes—from the outside there are similarities, but when closely examined, none of you are exactly the same. Your creation was not an easy process; on the contrary, very extensive thought went into making who you are, with special attention given to the smallest of details. You were created as a spiritual being. Your complete makeup and the essence of who you are is what we refer to as your Soul DNA. Your Soul DNA makeup includes a number of different things: gifts, talents, memory and free will are some of the more important ones. You were created in such a way that you can have access to all these important things when you need to. For example, you have been given the amazing ability, and the knowledge, of how to thrive wonderfully within your own physical or spiritual existence. You have access to this information when you are in the physical realm, yet it is rarely used.

Everyone's Soul DNA is different. There may be similarities, but the exact formula or combination is never the same. You have your own unique combination of gifts, talents and abilities, which help define who you are and give you your individuality. Since your Soul DNA contains such important information as the knowledge of how to be successful and how to heal the physical body, it is important for you to understand how and when you can access this vital information. You can access all this information and more when you are in complete harmony with your Soul DNA. For you to be in complete harmony, you must be able to maintain a good balance between your physical body and "etheric" body, or your spiritual body. When you have access to the information in your Soul DNA, you will have unlimited potential and amazing things will happen! As for your different talents and abilities, some of you may be stronger in some areas but weaker in others, and vice versa. The things that you experience and the knowledge that you acquire throughout all of your lifetimes also help define who you are. This is stored in your Soul DNA memory bank. No one has had the exact same experiences that you have had throughout all of your lifetimes, let alone this lifetime. Reincarnation is a large part of your Soul

DNA; you are a student of learning and you are here on earth to gather information for your own individual evolvement. It does not matter how fast you evolve or even how far you evolve; there are no set goals here, and it is not a competition. You create your own curriculum, you set your own pace and you set the extent to which you would like to continue to evolve or, to put it simply, to learn.

Regardless the extent to which we learn, we are all created equal and we will all remain equal. Each of us is a gift of God, created with love.

> *"Never compare your life to someone else's life.*
> *Your journey is unique and one of a kind.*
> *That's what makes your life special!"*

During each of your lifetimes, you will have different experiences and you will gain more knowledge; whether you remember it or not, it will become an imprint on your Soul DNA. When you are here on earth, you are attending many years of school, gathering as much knowledge as you can. Before each lifetime, you and your Spirit Guide carefully plan out your life path. You get to help with your lesson plan; you get to pick some of the classes that you take and almost all of your teachers. You do this by deciding what things you would like to experience while you are on your journey. Throughout each one of your lifetimes you will gather knowledge from all of your experiences and store it in your Soul DNA memory bank; it is then carried with you forever. This helps with your evolvement. Some of the knowledge that you gain and some of the experiences that you have will be positive and some of them will be negative. You began this learning process at the beginning of your creation, and you will continue to gather more imprints and memories until you no longer choose to reincarnate. Life is a continuous learning cycle and education for the Soul.

Some of the imprints you carry with you will have a direct effect on your perspective. Your perspective is the way in which you view things based on your experiences. This also helps define who you are. Since it is impossible for anyone else to have had the exact same experiences that you have had since your creation, other people's perspectives will differ from yours. Your perspective affects how you receive any new information. This is all a part of what makes you unique—you have different experiences, different perspectives and different relationships with some of the same people.

Your Soul DNA contains thousands of strands of amazing colors. These strands and colors all represent different information, different imprints and different knowledge. This knowledge is timeless information that is carried with you in your Soul DNA, which can be accessed at anytime. All the knowledge serves a purpose, to help you live your life to its fullest potential. When you live your life to its fullest potential, you are making the best use out of your visit here on earth. You are learning as much as you can and receiving the most valuable information.

How do you access this information? At the beginning of your creation, how to access this information was very fresh in your memory. You were very much in balance and in harmony with your Soul DNA. This was because the connection between your spiritual body and your physical body was very strong. This connection is what allowed early civilizations to be very advanced, much more so than they are today. Long ago, we were also given the knowledge of how to levitate, how to telecommunicate with each other and how to transport ourselves in many different ways. Most communication was done telepathically; though we had the ability to speak, we preferred to use telepathy. Levitation was used to create and build different structures, some of which are still standing to this day. This is the same information that we have access to today and the same information that is still a part of our Soul DNA. However, at this time most of us only use these abilities when we have released our physical body and have crossed over. When we go back to our natural state of existence, as spiritual beings in spirit form, we have total, unblocked access to our Soul DNA and the knowledge it holds. As spiritual beings, we then relax into our natural state of allowing after releasing ourselves from our physical body and the resistance that goes along with it.

Most people underestimate the importance of having a good balance between their spiritual and physical bodies while living in the physical world. Therefore, it is continuously overlooked and often ignored. People do understand that it is important to be in balance, but they do not understand how to achieve balance, or what being in balance really is. Being in balance, or being in harmony, is when our spiritual body and our physical body are working together as equal parts. Each one needs the other to help thrive successfully while here on earth. By referring to our spiritual body, it does not mean that you have to be religious; that is something entirely different. We are spiritually based. Our spiritual body is simply the essence of who we are; it is how we were created.

To help you understand this connection and how important it is to have your spiritual body and your physical body working together, I have an image for you: Imagine putting on a glove. Your hand represents your soul, or your spiritual body, because it is the essence of who you are. The glove represents the physical body because it temporarily covers the hand. Imagine that your glove is a perfect fit. When you slide your hand completely inside of the glove—because of the perfect fit—your hand and the glove are fully operational. With your hand inside, it is very easy to move the fingers of the glove. You can pick things up and have the full use of the glove because the glove and the hand are working together in harmony. If, on the other hand, you do not slide your hand completely inside of the glove but only partially inside, it is much harder to utilize the glove to its full potential. You can still move the glove around a bit, but you are very limited in what you can do, and you are much less successful in picking things up or using your fingers. Using your fingers becomes almost impossible because the material of the glove gets in the way. This is similar to what happens when your spiritual body and your physical body are not working together or they are not in complete harmony. To get the most that you can out of your physical body, you must be working in harmony with your soul or your spiritual body. This is because you are a spiritual being and eternal soul using the physical body temporarily to evolve, experience and to learn.

Over time, since the beginning of your creation, things began to shift. Negative aspects of the physical world began to overwhelm everyone's spiritual senses. Greed and selfishness became seductive. You were created with the ability to take physical form to experience free will, negativity, interaction and life on earth, among other things. Part of the reason this shift began to take place was because of free will. Throughout these early years, free will began to grow and evolve. Free will can be a wonderful gift; however, sometimes it can take on a whole different path in a negative direction. How you handle and utilize your free will, especially in combination with the other elements that are mixed in with your lives here on earth, is all a part of your evolvement and your learning process. At one point in time, the negative started to overwhelm the positive, and this created a problem. It was destructive, and this caused a "disconnect" between your spiritual body and the physical body, a kind of spiritual memory loss. It was the beginning of forgetting how to access your Soul DNA and the knowledge that was instilled within your spiritual genetic system.

To help us restore balance and harmony throughout those early years and even until now, many Spiritual Teachers have been sent. They have come and they have gone, but they will continue to come. These Teachers are all over the world at any given time, and they are trying to help by supplying information and knowledge on how to reconnect your spiritual body and your physical body and become more in balance. This has been a very long process, and there is so much more to learn and so much more to teach. At this time what most of us remember is such a small part of our own abilities. Our abilities are not lost; they are still accessible and will always be a part of our Soul DNA.

Most everyone has a very strong connection with his or her physical being and physical existence. In fact we live so completely in the physical world that it causes us not to be in balance, or in harmony, as whole beings. Since you have a strong physical connection already, if you can complement that with a strong connection to your spiritual side and your Soul DNA, there will be a noticeable difference. Your connection can be seen on an energetic level; it looks like the weave of a wicker basket. There are many variations and degrees as to how connected you are with your spiritual body, which is a part of your Soul DNA. Some people have a stronger connection than others and some people have a complete "disconnect." If there is a disconnect, this does not mean that your soul and your physical body are not connected, it means that they are not in balance. In other words, your spiritual body and your physical body are not working together in complete harmony, like the hand and the glove. You need balance and you need harmony to achieve optimal mental, emotional, physical and spiritual health. You came into this world in perfect balance, and you will leave this world and go back to being in perfect balance. The key is to achieve harmony while you are here on earth, while you are learning. It is not hard to do; your spiritual body and your physical body naturally crave balance. You need to understand that you have adapted yourself to a new set of physical rules since your birth, and these new rules have taught you nothing more than limitations. For you to find your balance and harmony, you will need to question your beliefs. You will need to question what you have been taught to believe is your reality thus far.

"Sometimes the Universe takes you in a direction that you are not sure you want to go. You think this when you can't see the destination. Stop the worrying and trust the Universe. It has roads to get you from one destination to another that you never even knew existed!"

Understanding Universal Laws

There Are Eighteen Universal Laws:

1) The Law of One or Oneness – Everything is connected, we are all one.

2) The Law of Vibration – Everything in the Universe vibrates, or offers a vibration.

3) The Law of Attraction – You attract into your life what you are offering vibrationally.

4) The Law of Allowing – The state of allowing is the purest state of manifesting. Allowing things to move without resistance and to evolve and grow naturally.

5) The Law of Resistance – Anything offering resistance will manifest itself into energy blockages, or stuck energy.

6) The Law of Detachment – This is the law of releasing or letting go from your desire.

7) The Law of Abundance – There is more than enough in the Universe, nothing is limited.

8) The Law of Intention – Directing energy as intention is the first step of creation and desire, which results in manifestation.

9) The Law of Action – Action must be taken in order to result in manifestation.

10) The Law of Cause and Effect – Every action has a reaction or a consequence.

11) The Law of Pure Potential – Everything and everyone is one of infinite possibilities.

12) The Law of Rhythm or Ebb and Flow – All things have a rhythm, a cycle, or an ebb and flow.

13) The Law of Polarity – Everything has an opposite to it, a yin and yang, complementary opposites as part of a greater whole.

14) The Law of Relativity – Everything has challenges or tests that they will face allowing them to find strength within.

15) The Law of Dharma or Purpose – Everything was created with a purpose.

16) The Law of Giving and Gratitude – The Universe dictates that you must give in order to receive.

17) The Law of Correspondence – The Universe, or reality, cannot contradict itself.

18) The Law of Love – Love is Universal energy in its purest most powerful state.

Universal Laws are incredibly confusing when we try to understand them purely with our logical mind. The good thing is that our Soul DNA "understands" the Universal Laws and has a natural understanding of how to work with them. Over the years, with our increased grounding and attachment to the physical world and the imbalance that this has caused, it has made our conscious memory of the Universal Laws very distant. Now, more than ever, we are in a place where we need to see something work in order to understand it or believe it to be true. If we cannot see it, it makes it hard for us to understand and easy to believe that it does not exist.

We believe in air, although we cannot see it, because we learned about it in school. Although, if you have ever been underwater, you have probably also experienced not having air. You also believe in gravity because you have seen pictures of the moon and what happens if there is no gravity. Most likely, though, you have never really been taught the Universal Laws. So that may make it hard to wrap your mind around the concept of being able to have so much control over your life and its outcome, whether it is with material things or with accomplishments. That makes it seem more like a fantasy, or too good to be true, since you were already taught your limitations! How many times have you heard the saying, "If it is too good to be true then it probably is"?

"Life is like a blank sheet of paper. You can view it like art, put it on an easel and create something amazing—or you can just carry it around with you as scratch paper and let people scribble whatever they want to on it."

The Universal Laws do indeed exist whether you know about them or not; whether you believe in them or not, they are in full operation. You do not think about the Law of Gravity, yet it is an important part of your everyday life. When you are working in harmony with the Universal Laws, your life will flow more fluidly. It is important to understand that when you are in harmony with the Universal Laws, whether you can see the outcome with your logical mind or not, things will always work out for the higher good. In other words, things will work out not just okay but in the best way possible for you. When you try to get involved and force a certain outcome that you think is best for you, life can become much harder than it needs to be.

"Imagine the Universe is a river. When you want something so badly, it is like trying to force the river to flow in a certain way. What you need to do is let go, take a ride on the river, and see where it takes you. You can choose the boat in which you ride, you can choose when to jump aboard, but you cannot change the flow of the river—it is too powerful!"

Now, when you are working with the Universal Laws, you are not on a boat ride to somewhere that you do not want to be. If you are on a road to somewhere that you do not want to be, this is something that you have had a hand in from the choices that you have made thus far. The Universal Laws work by creating the outcome that you are imagining, with your help. You are the creator of your own destiny! The Universe has no attachment to you or who you are. You give the Universe direction by way of mental pictures and images of what you want for the future; this is your direction to the Universe. The Universe then puts the wheels into motion for whatever your assignment was, in order to carry it out. You do not, however, have any control over the way that this assignment is carried out. This is because, a lot of the time, you cannot see, or you refuse to see, what is in harmony with your Soul DNA. So it is more of a team effort. You need to be willing to give a goal or direction by way of dreaming it, writing it or making pictures of what you want whether it is in your head or on paper. You are already doing this on a daily basis; you are sending out information to the Universe every day, whether you know it or not!

Many people have absolutely no direction and they feel completely lost. They do not feel as if they are getting anywhere, but this is because they have no plan. Not even a short-term plan! They just go through life day after day getting more frustrated and unhappy. This is what they are sending out into the Universe, frustration and unhappiness. The Universe takes the order and sends back to you, frustration and unhappiness. You really need to have an idea of what you would like to get out of life in order to get there. What makes you happy? What do you want to strive for? What you fail to realize is, what you are thinking about is going out to the Universe and creating your outcome, every single day.

> *"If you are confused about what you want to do in life, and you are undecided as to what path to take, don't be surprised when it feels as if you are going in circles. The Universe is a mind reader!"*

You may have been told repeatedly while you were growing up that you would never achieve what you wanted. Your dreams were way too unrealistic. If you believe this, then it is true; if you do not believe this, that is also true. There is unlimited potential in the Universe (The Law of Pure Potential), unlimited abundance in the Universe (The Law of Abundance), and you are already working with the Universal Laws everyday—it is in your Soul DNA! They are as much a part of how you operate as when you eat, breathe and walk. If you are skeptical about the Universal Laws, you really have nothing to lose. It does not cost you any money to create your future with pictures. It is powerful, beyond anything you can imagine! You can change your life just by recognizing the instructions that you have given the Universe in the past and consciously choosing to create a fabulous future—a future you could only dream about!

Do not get frustrated if you begin this process and do not see immediate results. It takes some time for certain things to materialize; you are not on your own timeline, you are on the Universe's timeline. Timing is everything, and you cannot always see all the other things that have to be in the right place at the right moment for the best possible outcome. If you would like to be one of those people who ignore the Universal Laws completely, here is what I suggest you do: nothing ... simply nothing! People do this all the time. You should complain about your situation, your life, your job, your relationship, and wait for something to change. Do nothing today, do nothing tomorrow, and nothing the day after that.

"People spend a lot of time waiting—waiting for opportunity, a new job, a direction or a sign. You can be a benchwarmer waiting to be put in the game or you can put yourself in the game and create opportunity. You cannot score a goal while you are sitting on the sidelines!"

It is amazing how long people will do nothing but simply wait, and they wait for years! A very key ingredient of the Universal Laws that many people miss is action (The Law of Action: Action must be taken for manifestation to occur). For your visualizing and for the mental pictures that you are sending out into the Universe to work, Universal Law dictates that you must take action! You must put some type of effort towards making your desires become a reality. Something, anything, because the Universal Laws respond to action!

"Opportunity will not knock on your front door while you are sitting at home waiting for something to happen, no matter how much visualizing you do! Opportunity will however greet you on the street if you are out in the world trying to make something happen!"

It's as simple as that! Action is so important for your future, and in all of the things that you do in your life. In so many ways, to be waiting and stagnant, to be uninvolved in creating your future, goes against your Soul DNA. This is so much so that if you choose to be stagnant, to only wait, your soul, in a sense, will become wilted. You will feel this in every part of your spiritual being and your physical body. Depression and unhappiness is a very large part of this path.

Another thing that is very interesting about benchwarmers is that they usually have just as much energy as anyone else, but they use it in a wasteful way. They use their energy judging what is going on in someone else's life, getting angry at the world, or chasing addiction. They have really decided that somehow their life is not going to work out the way that they wanted it to anyway, so why even try to get in the game.

"People spend an amazing amount of time worrying, feeling hopeless, being involved in family or friend drama and just waiting—without even realizing it. If they spent that same amount of time and energy enjoying life, thinking about and creating their future, success would be inevitable!"

Some people spend a lot of time and energy feeling sorry for themselves and being negative. They believe that everyone else has it better, and they wonder why they have it so rough. You would think that since they spend so much of their time waiting, they would have endless patience, but the opposite is true. They are very impatient and that is a big part of the problem. When they try to take action and to get in the game, they need to have almost instant results for their efforts. If this does not happen, which most of the time it does not, they go back to the bench complaining even more, and continue to wait.

"When hungry, if you wait for the fish to jump into your boat, you are going to starve to death. However, if you throw in your fishing line and imagine what a wonderful dinner you are going to have, the Universe will send many fish your way!"

Action gets the ball rolling, so to speak, with the Universe. It is a key component in creating opportunity. Never, ever limit yourself! This can also be a huge mistake with benchwarmers. They may decide, "Okay, I am ready to try this game thing again." But this time the problem becomes that they are so focused on getting one specific thing, like a specific job, or a specific house, etcetera, that they will literally put all of their "eggs in one basket." Then, like clockwork, if things do not work out exactly the way they wanted them to (The Law of Resistance), they become discouraged again and back to the bench they go.

If you choose to take action, you need to throw your limitations and your expectations out the window (The Law of Allowing), as to how you want something done and how fast. You have no control here; you are at the mercy of the Universe and its ebb and flow. Everything including the Universe has an ebb and flow to it (Universal Law: The Law of Rhythm or Ebb and Flow), you need to be flexible—not flexible so much in the destination or your ultimate goal, but flexible with the timing and the flow, or the route, in which the Universe will take to get you there. You cannot force the Universe to work faster; it does not matter one little bit how much you want something. That has absolutely no effect on the timing of the Universe at all.

"When you are relaxed about where you are at in life, things tend to flow more fluidly. It is as if you poke three holes in a bucket of water. The same amount of water is going to flow out the holes whether you let it flow or you shake the bucket. The difference is the amount of turmoil on the inside of the bucket!"

What you do have control over is the turmoil that you cause yourself in the meantime. If you can relax and be patient, you will be in better harmony with the ebb and flow of the Universe. Timing is a big part of the Universal Laws, and it is very important as to how and when things will work out.

This is something that you might as well just accept, that timing is everything. Imagine that there are rows and rows of dominoes. Imagine that they are all interconnected, that they are set up with obstacles and twists and turns, and the goal is to make them all come together, with the last one dropping into a cup. If all of the dominoes are not in place—say there is one or two of them missing or out of order—this will cause the flow to be incomplete, creating a delay; therefore, they will not come together as they should. Also realize that you cannot see all the dominoes from your position; all you can see is the cup. So you have no idea if the dominoes are in their proper place or not. Just like those dominoes, you are at the mercy of the Universe to make sure that the dominoes are all lined up and that the timing is right. Trust me when I tell you that there are hundreds of thousands of dominoes that need to be in place in order to make that one thing happen—a job you would not want! So here you are getting impatient and frustrated, when your only job at this time is to put your trust in the Universe. This is because there is no way for you to understand the timing. That is something that you were not gifted with in your Soul DNA. You have already created the cup by making the goal (The Law of Intention), and you have already taken action (The Law of Action); now your job is to hand your cup over to the Universe because timing is its specialty.

> *"Sometimes it can be so frustrating if you are not where you want to be in life. Hang in there—timing is everything. Just keep moving forward, goal in mind, and things will eventually fall into place."*

This does not mean that you cannot pursue other goals at this time. Just the opposite, in fact—now would be a great time for you to put your focus into creating more goals and more opportunities. This draws your attention and energy away from being frustrated (The Law of Resistance) and puts it into something more productive (The Law of Allowing). You should set big goals, little goals, short-term and long-term goals. What this does for you is it gives you a focus, something to work toward.

It is important to continuously be proactive in creating your future. What is really wonderful is that while you are off creating other goals and taking action with your trust in the Universe, out of nowhere you will hear the domino drop into the cup! Yes! Another goal accomplished! It feels great! Your job is to create the goals for your future and take action toward making those things happen. After you have taken action as far as you can go, if your goal has not yet been accomplished, hand it off to the Universe and go on to your next goal. It is a continuous cycle if you keep on goal setting. It is very fulfilling and almost magical when you get into the rhythm of things. When you begin to feel in harmony with the Universe, with its ebb and flow, your Soul DNA memory will start to come back. Then you will begin to work more naturally with the Universal Laws; it will become second nature, taking less effort.

Your Physical Body and Your Spiritual Health

Spiritual health is really something that needs to be acknowledged and definitely something that needs to be
maintained. Over the years people have lost touch with
their spiritual body, and this has created a huge problem. A problem because we are spiritual beings, having
a physical experience, on this earth. We were a spiritual
being before we came down to earth, we are spiritual
beings while we are on this earth, and we are spiritual
beings after we leave this earth. It is the essence of who
we are; it is our Soul DNA makeup. We are spiritual!

Many do not even know that spiritual health exists or even what it is. Since our creation we have started to go somewhat backward. We have so fully embraced our human experience, physical existence and free will that we have really lost the memory of how or what our spiritual self and spiritual health is.

You may believe that you were created first as a human with your physical body and that you will become a spirit after you cross over or release the physical body. If this is your belief, it means you really only have a sliver of information about your own existence and creation. We do not all of a sudden transform or vaporize into a spirit when we leave this planet. That would imply that a person is human first and a spiritual being second. You are the exact opposite. You were created as a spiritual being that has the ability to be born, have an earthly or physical experience, and then go back to the Other Side, carrying with you the knowledge and experiences from your journeys here on earth. Your Soul DNA holds a vast amount of knowledge that you need in order to run, maintain and heal the physical body. Most of these things are done on their own.

Both our spiritual body, as well as our physical body, have an impact on our overall health. Most of us address the physical side, as we should, but are not sure how the spiritual side plays a factor in our health and well-being, especially since we are not quite sure what the spiritual side of our existence is. We tend to think that our spiritual self is in our head, like a state of mind or a perspective of how we view things, or how close to God we are. Or perhaps it is the feeling that you get when you go to church. We do not understand that the spiritual side of us is the essence of who we are. It is the Soul DNA; it is what makes our existence on this earth possible. It is not separate from who we are; it is, just simply, our existence … period. When we neglect our spiritual side or do not understand what it is, we can lose touch with our spiritual health. When this happens, it can cause a disconnection between the soul and the body, therefore, with our Soul DNA and the valuable information it holds.

Happiness and perception, the pursuit of our gifts, the Law of Attraction, the understanding of Universal Laws, our intuition, vibrations—all these things play a part in our spiritual health and well-being. When we are in complete harmony with our Soul DNA, it will have a good effect on our overall health. This obviously does not mean that we are going to live here on this earth forever, or that we will never encounter people who have health issues as part of their own human experience or as part of their life path. But it does mean that for everyone, spiritual health is important and something that we do have total control over.

To maintain your spiritual health, one of the first things that you must do is to recognize and acknowledge that you have spiritual health. When you do this, over time, you may begin to remember and uncover memories of what your spiritual health is.

Secondly, it is important that you pay attention to the things in this book about creation, vibrations, etcetera, and work on being in harmony with your Soul DNA. These things together all have a great impact on your spiritual health and spiritual being, therefore, on your existence and how you thrive.

If you find yourself experiencing feeling disconnected between your spiritual self and your physical self, another thing that can be very helpful is when you go to bed at night, imagine your body and your soul intertwining and weaving back together, or reconnecting. You can do this at anytime of the day really, when you have a moment of free time. Feel the merge between your bodies and feel the charge and energy from the reconnection. Bask in this feeling for a while. Then continue to imagine the connection between the physical body and your spiritual body getting stronger and stronger, and imagine yourself as a whole being. This is a good time to release anything holding you back and replace it with strength, courage, calmness, more energy, or anything that you feel you need more of. Remember this feeling throughout the day and bring it to the surface again as many times as you can. Make this a routine at night and before you get out of bed in the morning. You should continue to do this until you feel as if you are fully joining your spiritual body and your physical body together, and that they are operating in harmony with one another. This in conjunction with acknowledging, and recognizing, that you are very much a spiritual being and that spiritual health does indeed exist will make a big difference. Spiritual health can really have a big impact on how you feel physically and emotionally. It was definitely part of the focus at the beginning of your creation, and it goes hand in hand with the physical body.

In the early years of humanity's creation, people began to separate the spiritual and the physical as if they were two separate issues. Spiritual health and spirituality became more of a religious event. Instead of simply being a part of who we are, it became more about control and power. Here is where free will came into the picture. As people fought for control, or power, fear became a usable tool. Spiritual health and spirituality became something different than what it really is. We were taught to believe that spirituality is something to aspire to, or that it is something we can receive if we do this, or don't do that. In some instances we were taught that it is a state of mind.

In reality, to become a spiritual being, we simply have to exist; it is who we are. We already have, and always will have, a deep connection to spirit and God, whether consciously aware of it or not. Someone does not give it to us; it is not earned; it is not lost or found; it is simply a part of who we are. It is a part of our Soul DNA. This connection was given to us at the beginning of our creation, and no one has a stronger or weaker connection; it simply is our connection. Over the years there has been an illusion created somehow that being spiritual is something separate from whom we are and is something to be reached, or sought after. This illusion has shifted our perspective and our views to make it seem as if it is indeed a separate thing, that being spiritual is something that we are, or something that we are not. If we view being spiritual as separate from simply who we are, or how we were created and the basis of our existence, it can cause a disconnection between our physical self and our spiritual self. Whether we are religious or not religious, whether we think about it or do not think about it, does not change the fact that we are a spiritual being first, having a human experience, and it is very much a part of our Soul DNA and, therefore, our existence.

To better understand the concept of spiritual health, let's look at it this way: Imagine that you have a glass of water. Imagine that you keep this glass of water outside, and you intend to keep it there for a long time. But you never tend to or acknowledge the water inside of the glass; you only focus your attention on the outside of the glass. You clean the glass and dust the glass. If the glass gets a chip in it, you repair it. When it rains outside, you dry it off so there will be no water spots on the glass. It always looks brand new from the outside. Since you are putting all of your focus and attention towards the outside of the glass, what do you think happens to the water inside of the glass? The water becomes green; bugs and dirt get into the water. The inside of the glass becomes slimy and discolored. The glass represents your body, and the water inside of the glass represents your spiritual self and your spiritual health. It makes no sense to deny or ignore maintaining the water inside of the glass; it is counterproductive. If you do, you are not maintaining the glass or the water to the best of your ability. The inside of the glass reflects the inside of your body and the different things that can go on when the water, or your spiritual health, is not being tended to. To maintain this glass of water to the best of your ability, all things need to be considered. The water and the glass are both important; however, the water is really the key, and if it is not properly cared for it has a huge impact on the glass.

> *"It does not matter if the glass is half full or half empty if the water in the glass is slimy and green."*

You see, the water is your spiritual self or spiritual body. It cannot be sought after or aspired to, and it is not acquired. The water is simply your existence. You were born with a full glass of water, and you will leave with all of the water with which you came, your entire spiritual being. No one can add more water, making you more of a spiritual being, or take some of your water away, making you less of a spiritual being; you will always remain the same. Since we are all equal, what makes the difference is the way in which your spiritual existence is cared for. So while it is important to maintain your physical health, it is equally important to maintain your spiritual health. To do this it is most important that you follow your heart and the gifts and abilities that were given to you at the beginning of your creation. It is important for you to understand what happiness is and to make a conscious decision to choose happiness. You can benefit even more by working with the Law of Attraction and the ebb and flow of the Universe. These things do affect your vibration and, therefore, your spiritual health and well-being. You are gifted with the tools to live a spiritually healthy existence. The process is very simple. You simply allow yourself to be guided by your heart center. The reason your heart and your heart center guide you is because you were created with love—this was also intentional in your creation.

The Gift of Free Will

You have been given free will to help you learn and evolve while adding individuality and by giving you choices. The individual choices that you make and the intent behind the choices you make will further define who you are. There are so many choices in life and so many different ways you can handle those choices. In addition there are consequences to the choices, and so on. This all adds a little bit more of a challenge to your life because it creates more grey areas. Everything is not black and white. It is shaded with many colors as to how you choose to handle something.

Many things that you experience on a daily basis will directly impact and utilize your free will. You have an abundance of choices every day that you need to make.

Most of you will make these choices without even thinking about them. You will choose, for example, where to eat, when to eat, what to buy, when to sleep, whether to be happy, whether to be angry, and whether or not to exercise. When you are really grounded in your physical existence, your emotions play a big part in how you will use your free will. They sway your choices without you being aware them.

Emotions such as judgment, temptation, greed, empathy and love will alter your perspective and guide your choices. This is not always a good thing. It can make things much harder, but this is all a part of the learning process. For you to use free will to the best of your ability, it is important that you are balanced when making choices. It is important that you are working with the Universe. You need to be able to remove your emotions to some degree and use your internal guidance system to help with your decision making. Your internal guidance system works with the ebb and flow of the Universe; your emotions do not. Emotions are based purely on your physical existence; therefore, they limit your ability and what you can accomplish. You can use your internal guidance system to help you make the smallest of choices to the largest of ones. It is not hard to do; on the contrary, it is very easy to do. Just ask yourself, "Am I making this decision because it feels right, because other people want me to, or because I have ulterior motives behind this decision?" Be honest with yourself. You are the only one who will know the answer, and the answer that works with the ebb and flow of the Universe is the one that feels right.

Free will has been given to you to help you achieve the most that you can out of your life experience. It is also there so that you can choose some of the routes that you will take on your life path. If free will was not a part of your Soul DNA, everyone would be the same. There would be no diversity, and diversity is a wonderful part of your experience here on earth. Free will is where you form your belief system and live your life accordingly, or not accordingly, to what you believe in. You need to have a belief system to help reflect what you are about and what it is that you stand for. You need to be able to make mistakes in order to learn from them.

> *"Judgment gives you a very good insight on what a person is really about. Not of the person being judged but of the person doing the judging."*

Judgment is a very good example of free will and how it reflects your or someone else's belief system. If you are judging someone else based on superficial issues, it says something about you. If you are judging someone's actions based on protection and love, that will say something about you in that regard. So free will, emotions and your belief system all make life a little more complex. It forces you to learn from your own experiences and from your own choices. It allows you to have consequences from your own choices, whether they are good or whether they are bad. Then it allows you to choose your reaction and make further choices. You can choose to see how your free will has affected your life or you can choose to ignore it. More free will! One of the wonderful things about free will is that if you have been making some choices that are not benefiting you, and you are going down a path that is not desirable, you can always use your free will and change your course.

"Where do you see yourself in five years if you continue going down the same road you are currently on? Are you happy with what you see? If not, now is a good time to jump in the drivers seat and take a different route!"

Before you were born you created a chart for yourself with all of the things that you wanted to experience and that which you wanted to learn. The purpose of you being here on earth and having those experiences is spiritual growth. Now there are a lot of things in your chart that you are meant to experience and learn from and some of those things you cannot change. How you handle those experiences in life and the choices that you make as a result of your experiences is where your free will comes in. For instance, with something like divorce or the passing on of a loved one, you have charted the major experience, but your choice on how you will handle your journey through this experience is up to you; it is your free will.

How will you handle the journey? Will you allow yourself to become incredibly depressed for years, choosing to be so unhappy that it is hard to function? Or will you use this experience and what you have gone through to gain knowledge to help others who are going through the same thing? What choices have you made? Do you make choices based on your emotions? How have you used your free will?

"Everyone experiences failure and disappointment in their life. What separates the people who achieve success and the people who do not? Two things—they have unconditional faith when others need a reason to believe and they are persistent."

Everyone has a main highway that they must travel, one they have charted before birth; it is called one's life path. This life path will take you from point A to point B, with several pit stops along the way. These pit stops are different experiences that you wanted to learn from during your lifetime. These experiences can be marriage, divorce, birth of children, health issues, etcetera. You can choose to take one of the main roads, which will have its ups and downs, curves, straight shots and even some resting areas, or you can choose to go off the beaten path, which is less traveled and definitely harder on your vehicle. Your vehicle represents your physical existence. If you choose the untraveled path, you may get lost, you may have breakdowns, and you may run into some dangerous situations. These side roads still route themselves in such a way that you will make all of the same pit stops along your life path that you are supposed to; however, the journey can be much harder. Taking the side roads is definitely a choice and it certainly involves free will. The wonderful thing is that at any point in time that you change your mind, you can always head back to the main road and continue on from there. That is also a choice.

Charting Your Life Path

Your life path is something that you and your Spirit Guides create together before you are born. Your life path is created with your Spirit Guides so that when you are here on earth, you have someone guiding you from the Other Side. They know all the things that you hope to accomplish throughout your lifetime experience. Your life path is sometimes referred to as your chart. It is basically the curriculum for when you come down to earth. It will include all of the things that you would like to experience while you are on your journey here on earth. When you are a young child, you do a very good job of starting your journey off on the right foot. Your spiritual body and your physical body are very much in harmony and in balance, so you are in tune with your Spirit Guides as well as the Universal Laws. This allows you to work very well with the ebb and flow of the Universe. The rules are really pretty basic and very simple; you are to follow the happiness in your heart. The heart center is usually where you can feel yourself being guided by your Spirit Guides. It is here that you can also feel when you are accessing your Soul DNA information. As a baby, since you still have a strong spiritual connection and memory of the Other Side, it is natural for you to plug into your Soul DNA and access its information. Naturally you are guided by happiness. If you take a moment and think back to when you were a child, you can usually remember that when you were growing up, you only did the things that you loved to do. It was usually something simple that brought you joy such as making mud pies, singing or playing dress up. This is the time in your life when you were blissful doing the things that you liked to do, and when you no longer enjoyed what you were doing, you just stopped and did something else. As a child, you base all of your decisions on what makes you feel happy and good in the heart center. If you watch little children, you can see how happy and carefree they are. It is not just because they do not have anything to worry about. On the contrary, some children have a lot of things on their mind, but they are coming from a different place. They are plugged into their Soul DNA, so they naturally make decisions from their heart center. They have a natural trust in the Universe that everything will always work out. Children spend most of their waking time doing things that make them happy. If these children were to follow their heart center throughout their entire life, as they got older, they would continue to discover and develop the gifts and talents that have been given as part of their Soul DNA. Ironically, most of the time the things that you loved to do when you were a child have something to do with what your gifts and talents are when you become an adult. When you follow your heart and what you enjoy doing, you are very much in harmony with your Soul DNA and your life path. In other words, one of the reasons that you enjoy doing certain things is because they are already a part of your Soul DNA. They are a part of who you are, otherwise you wouldn't enjoy doing them.

As you get older, however, you are introduced to many different perspectives and ways of thinking. These perspectives are usually from adults who have simply lost touch with who they are. They have lost touch with their own spiritual self and Soul DNA information. What was simply understood by you when you were young, now becomes confused with your mind and its logic. You are being taught to think about your decisions—think, think! You are taught about your brain and all the information that it holds and how to do things. You are being taught how the physical world works, given statistics and shown studies to give you more proof on how it all works. Everything you are taught is physically based; none of it is spiritually based. When you ask about the spiritual realm, you are told that it does not exist! You are told that it cannot be proven; it is not real. You are taught that dreams are just that, dreams. One of the worst parts is that you are told to stop daydreaming!

"Dreams are only dreams until they become reality
… Then they become that really amazing thing that
happened to you that day! Keep Dreaming!"

You are conditioned to believe that you have no control over your life path or the things that happen to you in your lifetime, that you are limited in what you can do and what you can accomplish, based on your abilities, your location, who you are, where you come from, et-cetera. What if you had grown up in a world that had never taught you such limitations? By that I mean, what if people never said to you, "You cannot run that fast. It's impossible!" Or, "How are you ever going to make that much money?" Your world would be completely different. You would have come from a world filled with unlimited potential and endless possibilities!

"The Universe and Spirit do not understand
limitations … PEOPLE invented limitations!"

When you are young you believe that anything is pos-sible because you are fresh from the Other Side. It is what you know; it is in your Soul DNA. You are born knowing the rules of the Universe, and the possibilities are endless! But when you get older, you are taught that this is not possible, and that is not possible. Your memory of the Other Side begins to fade, and you begin to learn a new set of rules, physical rules. You start to think that maybe here on earth, there are a different set of rules. You start to doubt the knowledge that came with you when you were born. When this happens you begin to doubt what you can accomplish. You begin to make more decisions based solely on the mind and its logic, with no input from the heart center. The heart center is a part of your spiritual connection and your Soul DNA, and therefore, it holds valuable information. It is good to make decisions with the mind based on its logic; however, there needs to be a balance between the mind and the heart center. When you solely use the mind, you begin to lose your spiritual connection. The spiritual connection is not felt in the mind, it is felt in the body.

When you become an adult, money becomes a major issue and a part of your everyday life. You begin to realize that you need money for everything. You need money to pay your bills. You need money to buy a house and feed your family, and those are just the basics. This causes you to have a shift in your perspective and a shift in your focus, so you begin to do what everyone else does—you try to bring in the best income that you know how.

"Fear is driven by people who do not truly understand the Laws of the Universe. Because if they did, they would understand that you get whatever you focus upon, whether it be fear or abundance … There will be plenty to go around!"

When money becomes a major focus, it drums up many different emotions such as jealousy, greed and unhappiness. Jealousy sets in when you begin desperately wanting what someone else has. This will cause you to begin making choices based on those emotions. You start to believe that there is only so much business to go around and so much money to be made. You begin to work at places that you hate. Your blood pressure gets higher, stress becomes a factor, and depression sets in. These things can all cause you to have health issues. You start competing with others. By this time your focus has shifted in the complete opposite direction of the Universe. Your focus should be on trying to live your life to its fullest potential and seeing what you can accomplish with the Universe. When you are working in the opposite direction of the Universe, you are working in a world completely structured by limitations. It is like trying to swim upstream. It is hard and exhausting, and you never seem to get anywhere! The people who have taught you limitations truly believe that you are limited, because they themselves are limited. So that is what they teach—they teach what they know. This is what they have been taught their entire life, and this is a cycle that you need to break. When you are living in a world full of limitations, it makes it harder to keep a positive attitude and it makes it harder to see the light at the end of the tunnel.

> *"Just because you cannot see the light at the*
> *end of the tunnel does not mean that it is not*
> *there. Maybe your tunnel has a lot of curves in*
> *it and the light is right around the corner!"*

Those of you who do not believe in limiting yourselves and those of you who are in harmony with your Soul DNA will have a whole different experience. You will have success where other people fail and where other people did not think it was possible.

> *"You finally see the light at the end of the tunnel,*
> *find your way out ... another tunnel ... this time*
> *grab a flashlight (makes things easier) ... start*
> *over again! You can never avoid more tunnels.*
> *The key is to get smarter with each one!"*

Records are broken when you are not restricted by other people's limitations whether they be athletic, financial or at the box office. You need to understand that the Universe has a whole different set of rules. When you see past all the limitations, doors open for you where before there was only a wall. Without even trying you will meet people who want to help you accomplish your goals. There is more success, happiness and wealth in the

Universe than you can possibly imagine! It is abundant! There are no limitations; there is plenty for everyone. When you really begin to understand this, there will be no jealousy. You will begin to understand that you should help everyone achieve their dreams to the best of your ability. When you do this, people will come "out of the woodwork" and help support you in your success!

A very important key to help you through your life path is simply to follow what gifts and abilities you have been given. In other words, follow whatever it is that you enjoy doing. It sounds simple, doesn't it? Many times I hear people say, "Well how do I know what my gift is?" What is it that you enjoy doing most in life or have the most passion for or interest in? If you can answer that question, you have found your gift! It is something that you enjoy doing so much that when you are doing it, you lose track of time; something that you would most likely do anyway; for free. You are usually gifted in areas that are of great interest to you. You know what your interests are and you know what you enjoy doing, so now you know that somewhere in that area is your gift.

"Every one of us is born with a unique gift that nobody else has. It is unique because you are the only one with that particular gift. It is your job to figure out the gift you have been given and develop it. This is what makes your soul in harmony with the Universe. It could be in teaching, sports, writing or talking with people. What is your gift?"

Your gifts are all very valuable, and you will be led down a wonderful life path when you follow your heart and pursue those gifts. If you love putting outfits together for your friends, you should consider styling. If you love to play golf but cannot make the PGA tour, look into working at a golf resort. If you love talking with people, do not find a job behind a desk; find something where you are interacting with people. If you love music, but you cannot sing, there are plenty of other jobs in the music industry. Do not limit yourself, but do keep within the area of your passion! If you do this, you will come into harmony with your Soul and therefore with the vibration of the Universe.

Who Are Your Spirit Guides?

Before you are born, you choose someone from the Other Side to help guide you through the experiences that you will have here on earth during your lifetime. These spirits are what we refer to as your Spirit Guides. Your Spirit Guides are spirits that have incarnated before. When they enter into an agreement with you, however, they will stay on the Other Side for the entire time that you remain in the physical realm. Everyone has at least one main Spirit Guide who works closely with him or her on a day-to-day basis. The Spirit Guide that I am referring to is not an animal, or your grandma or your grandpa. If your Spirit Guide was someone that you knew while you were here on earth, that would mean that at some point in time you would have been here without any guidance from the Other Side, and that is just not the case. They are with you from the day you are conceived and they stay with you until you release your physical body.

Some of you think that your Spirit Guide is not around you or that you do not have any interaction or communication with them. You think that if you do not hear them, sense them or feel them that they simply do not exist. Sometimes you have just blocked your ability to receive guidance from them or you think that it is just your imagination. Communicating with your Spirit Guides or receiving information does not have to be taught to you. It is built into your Soul DNA, allowing you to have a natural ability to be able to receive guidance from them. So you do not have to learn or train yourself how to do this; however, you do need to be more aware of how you receive this information. It is also important to have an understanding of how this communication system works. You have something similar to an internal antenna or an internal connection to the Other Side and to your Spirit Guide. It is always there, and your connection can always be accessed. Your Spirit Guide is trying to guide you and communicate with you all of the time, but most of the time, you do not even notice it. You may be under the impression that when your Spirit Guide talks to you, that you should be able to hear them as you do when you are having a conversation with someone in the physical realm. So if you do not hear them, you think that there is no communication with your Guides. Some of you also believe that it is something that you must work very hard at, with meditation or by sitting quietly in a room by yourself. In some instances that can definitely help further your level of communication, but for the most part, this is not necessary. Most psychics and mediums do not hear their Spirit Guides with the outer ear, as you would hear a friend talking to you. They hear with their inner ear and you can do this too. When you hear with your inner ear, it is like remembering a conversation that you had with someone yesterday, or replaying a song in your head that you just heard on the radio. Those are good examples of what hearing with your inner ear is like. Your Spirit Guides can contact you and say things aloud, or audibly, so that you can hear them with your outer ear; however, this is rarely the way in which they will communicate. I have had this happen to me on a few different occasions and it is quite jarring! The first time it happened, I was a lot younger, and for a moment I was frozen with fear. My Guides tell me that they do not like to communicate in this way for this exact reason; it can be quite startling and very scary. Your Spirit Guide will most likely communicate with you through pictures and telepathy. It is usually through pictures or a "feeling" that you get in your stomach or somewhere in the body, or an image that you will get in your head. The problem with picture communication is that sometimes there are symbols, and you need to figure out what the pictures or symbols mean to you. For instance, they may show you a particular color of flower, and that flower will mean something. Also when they communicate with you telepathically, you tend to question whether they are your Spirit Guides or if you are just making something up in your head. One easy way that you can usually tell the difference is that if you are actually hearing or receiving information from your Spirit Guide, you will feel it in your body, not just your mind. This is because you are raising your vibration and connecting with your spiritual body or your Soul DNA. This is your internal connection. You will usually feel it in your heart center, the same place that you can feel your intuition. Sometimes you can feel it in your stomach, like a "gut feeling," or in the back of your neck. Whatever way, there will be a noticeable feeling in your body.

When you realize that you are getting messages from your Spirit Guide, you need to pay attention to the pictures and symbols that are being sent to you. You need to figure out what they mean to you, and this will help you understand what they are trying to say. You need to pay attention to the telepathic messages that you are hearing or seeing, and notice the feeling that you have in the body. This will heighten your awareness. When you start to notice the connection between your spiritual being and the physical body, it will become even stronger. With practice your communication can advance.

You have probably experienced such a situation or heard a story similar to this one. For example, you have been driving the same way home from work or school day after day. But one day you have a strange feeling not to go the same way that you always go, so you take a different route. Later you hear that there was an accident on the street that you normally take home. That would be your Spirit Guides giving you a "feeling" to take another route. This is their way of helping to divert you from a dangerous situation. This can also happen with small things, such as if you are driving down a rode slightly over the speed limit and a car gets in front of you. This car is driving exactly the speed limit, and you proceed to cuss them out because you are in a hurry. Then about a mile down the road, you pass a police officer and realize that you just avoided a speeding ticket, and you really did not need to be driving over the speed limit anyway.

Spirit Guides and the Universe work well together because they are in complete harmony, and your Spirit Guide is completely in sync with the Universal Laws. They are guiding you with an array of knowledge from the Other Side and with Universal Laws in mind.

"When you receive a lot of advice from friends/ family, it sways your perspective and it can take you away from your own internal guidance system. If you were driving and became lost, would you turn on your perfectly working GPS system and follow it? Or would you leave it off, call your friend and say, "What does your GPS system say I should do?"

Here is a good example of how your Spirit Guides are helping to guide you with your best interest in mind, especially when you are not on the right path or when it is affecting your spiritual being in a negative way. Years ago I was working in a place that was just horrible for me. The woman whom I worked for was mean and depressed. She thought that everyone from employees to salespeople should cater to her. I had customers who constantly wanted to complain to the manager about how rude she was. So it was terribly embarrassing when we had to explain to them that she was the owner! It was not a good situation, and nightly I would imagine working somewhere that was a better fit for me in the future, somewhere that I loved. One day she called a meeting with me, where she told me that she was going to cut my hours in half! I was surprised. Since I had taken a pay cut when I started the job, I told her that I did not think that I could afford to work part-time. I let her know that if she was going to cut back my hours, I might need to look for another job. She was visibly irritated and told me to take the rest of the day off. I worked there for about two more days, and then I was fired! Even though a month earlier I had received a written note about how well I was doing. It was quite a shock, and to say the least, I was very upset! I needed an income, so I immediately applied for unemployment and began looking for work. About a month went by, and one of the workers from the unemployment office told me that there was an ad in the newspaper she happened to see that she thought I would be very qualified for. She told me where to look; it was something that I never would have found on my own. The job seemed like a good match, so I applied. I went in for two interviews and I ended up being hired at the company, but not in the position that I had applied for. The company had created a new position for me that was even a little better than the one for which I had originally applied. I loved it! It had health insurance, a 401K plan and paid vacations. I had none of these things at my previous job. This is a very good example of my Spirit Guide helping me to achieve a better situation. Had I not been fired, I would have not met the lady at the unemployment office. Therefore, I would not have heard about my new job and would not have been able to apply, not to mention who knows how long I would have had to put up with the terrible situation I was in.

We can definitely be stubborn and not listen to our Spirit Guides or the Universe. When I look back, there were several signs that I should have moved on sooner. I was so stressed out that my health was being affected. I would come home every day unhappy. I was working with people who were not nice people. Since I was not listening to my Spirit Guide, extreme measures were taken.

When things do not work out the way we want or had hoped, there is usually a good reason. We will just not understand why until later on down the road. Some good examples would be if you did not get a job that you really wanted, or a loan fell through. Instead of trying to see what the reason might be, or recognizing that for some reason it was not right for you at that time, you might become really frustrated and upset.

Imagine that you are in this maze called life, blindfolded, and you have to find your way to the end. This maze does not only have corners, but it has bumps in the road and several obstacles along the way. Your Spirit Guides are like the people above in the lookout tower; they can see the whole maze. They can see where you need to go to get to the end and the best route you can take to get there; they are a part of your team. If you listen closely and pay attention to the signs they give you, they can help you maneuver corners and steer clear of the obstacles. They can warn you when a hill is coming and help you to avoid bumping into walls. They come when they are asked, and they stay as long as they are needed. But when you are not listening, and you think that you can make it through this maze all on your own, it is much harder. If you start veering too far off the path or too far from your destination, sometimes they must take extreme measures. They can box you in or put up a wall in order to make you turn around. This will get you back on the right track, going in a direction that is right for you. But, at this point, you may be too angry or focused on that wrong direction to notice that you are being helped. It may not be until you are further down the road that you are able to look back and see why you were rerouted.

"If you tend to be running into a lot of road blocks lately, try a different path; don't just give up. The Universe will sometimes put a road block in your path to get you to take a different route, not necessarily to change your destination."

A lot of times, children will see their Spirit Guides or feel their presence around them. As adults, we can sometimes feel their presence too, but it tends to freak us out. We can feel them behind us, over one of our shoulders or in our car. It feels as if someone is standing behind us, but when we turn around, there is no one there. That is usually our Spirit Guide. In fact, when my son was very young, he would often see his Spirit Guide who would be walking on the front porch of our house or would show up at the end of his bed. My son knew what he looked like; he would tell me what Frank, his Spirit Guide, would be wearing. Most of the time when he would see Frank, it would be at night. This is very common because the veil between the physical realm and the spiritual realm is thinner at night, and we are more open to seeing things because of the alpha state we are in prior to falling asleep. I know that this tends to freak people out, but it did not scare my son. He knew that it was his Spirit Guide, and he knew that Frank was there to watch over him. One night, shortly after I had asked my son if he knew why his Guide was always walking on the front porch, his Spirit Guide started talking to me. He sounded as if he was on a radio station that was mostly tuned in but a little fuzzy. I asked him what his name was and he said, "Frank." This is how we got the name, in case you were wondering. So then I asked him why he was here, and he said, "I am here for protection." He was answering my own questions, since my son had already known this to be true. It was quite amazing and informative at the same time. My son still has a strong connection with Frank, and although he does not appear all of the time, he makes his presence known every now and again. It is nice to know that he is always around.

A lot of writers and musicians get their ideas and information through their Spirit Guides. Most of the writing I do and the information I receive is from my Spirit Guides; they are my Spiritual Teachers. When I started writing articles, I would be flooded with information. It was as if I were listening to someone in the room and writing down what I was being told, as in dictation. This process began to flow so nicely that I could sit down and write a whole article in an hour. I would never read what I was writing until the article was finished. Then I would go back to correct any typing errors and read the article in its entirety. It was fun for me because I would always think, "Wow, that was really interesting!" I would rarely have to reword things or edit much. After I mastered that technique for a while and things started to flow extremely well, I started receiving more and more information, and that is the information that is in this book. This type of channeling, or receiving of information, is also very common with musicians who compose their own music. It feels very different when I am receiving information from my Spirit Guides and writing than when I am engaged in other types of writing. When I am receiving information from my Guides, as I mentioned before, I can feel it in my body. It also feels as if I am in a "zone" so to speak, and the information just flows out with ease. It is a very calm and relaxed feeling that comes over me.

Spirit Guides are also different from your Guardian Angel. Your Guardian Angel has a very specific task and that task is to protect you. They can also intervene if you get yourself into a potentially harmful situation. Here is a story about an encounter that my son had with his Guardian Angel. One day my son was swimming in the backyard of his grandma's house. She was inside at the time and the grandchildren were outside playing. He was about five years old, and while he was playing around the swimming pool, he fell in. The pool was not very deep, but when he fell into the pool, it was at an awkward angle, and he could not make his way to the top. The other kids did not seem to notice. Right when he thought that he might drown, he felt someone grab him by the arms and stand him straight up onto his feet. As he was telling me this story I began to panic on the inside. "Who grabbed you?" I asked. "It was my Guardian Angel," he said. "Did you see her?" I asked. "Yeah," he said, "and then she disappeared!" I cannot tell you how relieved I was by that intervention. He is much older now, but he still sees her every now and again hovering about his bed while he is sleeping.

Your Spirit Guides also can be protectors, but they are mostly around for guidance; your Guardian Angel is here specifically to protect you. Either way it is wonderful to have a team help guide and protect you. It is even more wonderful when you are an active participant on the team. It makes your team that much more successful!

Career and Money Flow

It is painfully obvious how unhappy many of you are in the workplace. It does not necessarily have to be because of your work environment or even because of the people with whom you work, although it can be. Mostly your unhappiness stems from what is called career incompatibility. When you create a mental checklist for a job, money is usually at the top of the list. You do this automatically because in the back of your mind, you are thinking about all of your responsibilities, and most of those require that you have money. When you are thinking purely from a logical mindset, with the limitations you have been taught thus far, it seems logical. Your logical mind does not take into consideration your Soul DNA and the Universal Laws. Your logical mind is practical and fear based; it includes all the physical rules.

It means that most of you are not making a career choice while being in balance or in harmony with your Soul DNA. If your mental checklist was made while you were in balance with your spiritual side, your list would have some of these items in reverse order. At the top of your list would always be doing something that you love to do or that you enjoy doing. In other words, using your gifts and talents given to you in your Soul DNA. When you understand how the Universe works, especially when you are in harmony with your Soul DNA, you understand that this harmony has a direct effect on your money flow. If you choose your career based on passion, money will follow; it is as simple as that.

> *"When looking for a job, if you search for something based on your passion and what you enjoy, money will be sure to follow. If your search is based on money or desperation, stress will be sure to follow."*

Since you spend about forty percent of your waking time at work, why do you choose your work or place of work so carelessly? Because the majority of you hold onto your physical beliefs and find it hard to believe that you can actually get paid for doing something that you like to do or that you love to do. That just seems unrealistic, especially since most people whom you know do not love what they do. So, you are limited. You are limited in what you look for and limited in what you believe is available to you; therefore, you have limited opportunities. As you begin searching for work, you go about it all wrong, placing money at the top of the list. This usually results in incompatibility; and when there is incompatibility, unhappiness will follow. When you look for work by looking in the newspaper to see what jobs are listed and what pays the best, your options are limited. What you do not understand is the relationship that your money flow has in relation to the Universe, and how the Universe can open up doors for you if you just take a leap of faith.

Some of the best jobs I ever had were when I was suddenly out of work, through no fault of my own. Once when I was younger, I was laid off from a place that I had been working for several years. This made me nervous because of obvious reasons, the drop in income. I was not even sure where to start looking. Since I was younger, I did what everyone else did; I took a mental inventory of what my qualifications were and where I might find the best paying job. Then my husband said to me, "Why don't you just figure out where you would most like to work and apply at those places." After some thought, I said, "Well, they probably won't be hiring!" His response was what changed my perspective and instantly brought me back into balance with my spiritual self and Soul DNA. "How do you know? Have you called them?" Well, no, I had not called anyone because up until this point I had been looking in the newspaper, assuming that those job listings were all of my options. After I shifted my perspective and began to get back in touch with my heart center, I did some thinking. Many ideas came to mind, and I changed the priorities on my checklist.

At the time I happened to love football, and I knew quite a bit about the sport. About four months before I had been laid off, a new professional indoor football team had started up in our town. I thought to myself, "I would love to work there!" But, it had been a while since they had opened, and I was sure that all the openings had been filled. I was curious though, and something told me to call and inquire about openings anyway, so I did. When I called I was shocked to find out that they were just starting to look for an office manager. I was very qualified for this position and I was asked to come in for an interview. After a meeting with the general manager and the assistant general manager, I was feeling pretty good. I was not only feeling good about the interview but how I changed the way I was going about looking for work. After a few days had gone by, the general manager called and offered me the job! I couldn't believe how easy that was! This had all happened within about two weeks of me rearranging my mental checklist. What a wonderful opportunity! If I had not been laid off, I wouldn't have taken my leap of faith!

This story gets even better. I was hired at a salary a little less than I was used to, but I was so happy to work in a place of huge interest to me that I was fine with it. I now had to work on weekends, which I had never done before because that was the time I spent with my family. But I figured that it was for only four months out of the year, and it was worth it to me to work somewhere that I enjoyed, so I was okay with that too. After about a month or so as the office manager for the new football team, the general manager had a heart issue, and this set off a chain of events. He was in and out of the hospital and was eventually told by his doctors that he could not continue to work there any longer because of the stress of his particular position. The assistant general manager had decided he did not want the general manager position. So he put in his two weeks notice and went to work somewhere else he enjoyed much more. (This is a very good example of a job being incompatible with one person's happiness yet very compatible with someone else's.) So guess who was next in line! I went from being the office manager to general manager of the new indoor football team in less than two months, with more than double the salary I was making at my last job! I was even able to involve my family by having them help me on the weekends, volunteering their time, which was something that they enjoyed. That resulted in even more family time and some really great memories. I could not have asked for anything more! This was a dream job for me, and in my wildest dreams I could not have seen this coming. If I had continued along the same path of job-hunting that most everyone does, I would have missed this amazing opportunity. The Universe works in harmony with you when you are in harmony with your talents and with your passion. At this time the Universe did not just open doors, it laid out the red carpet right in front of me! I am obviously no longer at that job; eventually I outgrew it and moved on to something else. But I enjoyed it immensely, and I made some amazing friends. One of them is still a very good friend of mine even to this day. It is funny because one of my favorite things to do when I was younger was to pretend as if I were running an office. Now that is a good example of remembering your Soul DNA—thanks to my husband!

When you remember what it is that you enjoy doing so much, never think that it is something that you cannot pursue and make money at in some way. There are many paths and different areas to all kinds of careers, not just one. If you are in a career that you enjoy, but you are not as far as you would like to be, do not get frustrated. Timing is everything! Remember the chapter on Universal Laws? Also, never compare yourself to other people and think that you are not as good or talented as this person or that person. Never doubt your gifts. Remember that none of you have the exact same gifts or talents and that you are on your own journey. No one is better than you; they are just different than you. If someone is better known in their craft than you, that certainly does not make them better. It just means that their path is different from yours. Another important key here is to remember that not everyone is supposed to be famous in his or her field of choice, nor should everyone want to be. Many people believe that fame is how you can judge if you are good at what you do. Happiness means different things to different people. Most do not see the downside to being famous—the demand on your time, the loss of privacy, or the pressures that it brings. Being successful is having a happy heart because you enjoy what it is you are doing and how you are spending your time. Working at something you enjoy does amazing things for your spirit, and when you are in harmony with your spiritual self or your Soul DNA and the Universe, happiness and money will follow! The fulfillment is wonderful and the income potential is limitless. If you are unhappy in your job or you are looking for a new job, take a leap of faith! It may seem like a huge leap, but if you do not try, you will never be able to walk on your red carpet.

"You were carefully created, and you were instilled with the ability to be successful in a career that you love. You are unique and one of a kind, and your gifts and abilities are special to only you. Every one of you was created with greatness in mind. Never, ever doubt yourself or your ability to achieve success ... God never did!"

The Pursuit of Happiness

More and more of you are increasingly unhappy with your job, your finances and your relationships, or unhappy with life in general. There has been a huge shift over the years with how happy people are, and even more importantly, with how everyone defines happiness. This is really kind of sad when you understand what happiness truly is. Happiness is a gift from God! It is a wonderful feeling that has been given to you, and you can choose to access it at any time. When and how often you use this amazing gift is up to you! You can choose to access it all day everyday and live your life in complete bliss, or you can choose to ignore it or save it and only bring it out for special occasions; it is your own personal choice.

"Every single day of your life you can find one or more reasons to be unhappy. Happiness is not bought, given, earned or learned. It is a state of mind based on your perspective. Happiness is simply a choice ..."

Since you already hold the tools to your own happiness, it is really amazing how many of you are unsatisfied or unhappy with your own life. It is very apparent that most of you no longer understand what true happiness is. You wait and wait for your life to change in order to be happy. When you are at this point, when you have really lost touch with your Soul DNA and what true happiness is, it makes things even harder. Happiness is a state of mind based on a perspective, your perspective. It is really that simple. This explains why you can see someone who, despite being in unfavorable circumstances, remains a very happy person, and how you can see someone who really has a pretty good life but is miserable all the time. When you feel unhappy, you begin to search for happiness in all the wrong places, as if it can be found somewhere. You turn to someone else to make you happy, whether it is your husband, your wife, your girlfriend, your boyfriend or your children. Their behavior is somehow directly linked to your happiness.

"You would not want to be responsible for someone else's happiness, so please do not hold someone else responsible for yours!"

You need more money and a better job to be happy. You need more than one vacation a year, and it has to be in a very wonderful place since you are overworked. As if being overworked and underpaid is not enough, you have to come home and deal with your partner. You are tired of dealing with the drama, the fighting and all the unhappiness in your relationship. If only your partner would behave as you wanted, treated you better, or gave you more support, then ... you would be happy!

"Unhappiness can be like a virus spreading from one person, to the next person, to the next one and so on. When someone is mean or rude to you, do not let their unhappiness infect your own life. If you are the unhappy one, please quarantine yourself so you do not infect others!"

You have heard it all before, that you need to find happiness within yourself before you can be truly happy. Most people say, "Great, but I have no idea what the heck you are talking about. I worked all day, and I have to make dinner—no thanks to my significant other! I am too tired to even try." You become more frustrated and more unhappiness sets in. You begin to feel lost and lash out in many different areas of your life. You are sure this thing or that thing is definitely the cause of your unhappiness.

Not once do you stop and check your internal view of the world, or your perspective. That would make you feel as if you might be part of the problem, part of the cause of your unhappiness! You think, "It is certainly not my fault!" So why would you check your own internal view? It also does not occur to you because happiness feels as if it is received from outside of yourself somewhere. You do not even give it a second thought! You think that something or someone showers you with happiness, so to speak. This is kind of like when someone says that happiness came over him or her. You do not even take the time to realize that your reaction to something or someone is all internal; and since it is all internal, it is all based on your perspective, or your internal view. Since your perspective is under your control and your control alone, happiness is a choice, your choice. It is not given to you by someone or something; the choice is a part of your free will. Happiness was gifted to you by God in the creation of your Soul DNA.

Many of you tend to link your happiness or unhappiness to your relationships or to your job. You believe that you are underpaid, overworked and underappreciated. It is no longer a gift to have a job or to be satisfied that you are paid consistently week after week. You want more money, more status and more recognition. It is also no longer enough to be responsible for your own self-esteem and who you are, it is more important that other people view you as wonderful too. You want them to recognize what a wonderful person you are and what a great employee you are. That makes you feel good; in fact, you think that it makes you happy! You need money to spend on more things to make you happy—a boat, a new car, a bigger place (because the place that you live in now is definitely too old, too small and too far away). Instant gratification has replaced true happiness. The problem with this is that instant gratification is very short lived, and the next thing you know is that you are feeling unsatisfied, trying to find happiness again; it is like an addiction.

"When working with the Universal Laws you are working with the laws of manifestation not instant gratification ... "

This is not even remotely close to what true happiness really is! It is not the promotion to buy more things. It is not the best new gadgets on the market. It is not the best clothes for your kids or the luxurious lifestyle. A luxurious lifestyle reflects happiness, you think, so this is what you strive for. What you do not understand is that living a luxurious lifestyle will not make you happy, especially if your perspective and internal view stay the same. Happiness and unhappiness come in all sizes, in all income brackets and exist in all parts of the world.

You are really beginning to relate happiness to technology, more instant gratification. If someone were to take away your cell phone, most of you would feel instantly unhappy. Because you would no longer be in possession of what you view as your lifeline, and your connection, to everything that makes you happy. The cell phone is not the core of your happiness. Your "perception" of the cell phone and what it does for you is where your happiness stems from here. If you spent half of your time trying to make that same connection with your spiritual being and your Soul DNA as you do trying to stay connected with the outside world, your life would change dramatically.

You also mistake the feeling of being "unsatisfied" with the feeling of being "unhappy." Being unsatisfied and being unhappy are not the same thing. If you are unsatisfied with where you are at in life, this is a wonderful gift or sign from your Soul DNA. It is a signal for you to make a change, a change for the better. When you are feeling unsatisfied you should begin to get excited and keep your eyes peeled for opportunities. Because if you are in tune with your Soul DNA enough to recognize that this is a sign to move in a new direction, the Universe will offer you some choices. The key here is to be aware—to be aware that it is time to make a change and to be aware that opportunity is coming. This is also a good time to pursue and take action on finding opportunity, not to just sit and wait. If you take action (The Law of Action), you will see much faster results.

"Action is a key component to the Law of Attraction. Trying to makethe Law of Attraction work for you without taking any action toward your goal is like having a car with an empty gas tank. It may start up on fumes, but it is not going to take you where you want to go."

Finding happiness in yourself is not a chore, and it does not require you to take a self-help workshop to crack the secret code of happiness. You already have the knowledge in your Soul DNA, and it costs you nothing. It was a gift! Happiness is simply a state of mind based on a perspective, your own perspective. It is not a house, a car or a boat. It is not a large salary, a job promotion or status; it is a state of mind. People have really lost touch with being able to see the good side of things and appreciate what they do have. Everyone has become too focused on what they don't have. You can be happy no matter what job you have, no matter how big your house is or what shape your car is in. There are terminally ill children who experience tremendous happiness and have an appreciation for life. They have made the conscious choice to be happy; they understand what true happiness is. They make the absolute best out of the gift they have been given; this is amazing and inspirational at the same time. You can choose to see things through negativity and unhappiness, or you can choose to change your perspective—it's as simple as that.

Here is a story that shows how a simple change in your perspective can change your situation. Jenna was becoming increasingly unhappy at her place of work. Her job was in the junior clothing section of a large department store. She was actually going to college to pursue her degree in fashion. The job had flexible hours, health benefits, an employee discount and it was close to her house, so it only took her about five minutes to get to work. Since she had been working there for a while she was also included in the weekly management meetings. The management team thought that she had a valuable opinion regarding fashion and what was going on in the store. Fashion was something that she loved and it was an industry in which she enjoyed working. But as time went on, the same job that she loved so much before began to aggravate her. She did not feel as if there was much room for advancement, and even if there was, she was not really sure that was what she wanted. Jenna no longer appreciated all the things that she loved before. Her perspective had changed, and she became increasingly unsatisfied, until she decided to look for another job. When she found another job, she put in her two weeks' notice and left on good terms.

The next place that Jenna went to work was at a high-end retail store. She had beat out one hundred other applicants for this position. It was a better paying job with commission. Many girls wanted to work at this particular store because of its popularity. It seemed like a dream job; however, it quickly turned out to be more like a nightmare. The employees were very self-absorbed and one of the managers was in constant competition with Jenna for top sales. Her sales were very high, and this clearly did not sit well with him. He began to make rude comments such as, "Why would you wear your hair like that?" The more people pointed out that Jenna was outselling him, the more awful and rude he became. Other employees were also not very nice and would make comments to her about her size seven frame. Jealousy in the air stirred up nasty emotions and made for an unpleasant workplace. The money was better, but there was no insurance. The drive to work took about a half hour on good days and up to an hour on bad days. This was not at all what Jenna had imagined. During this time she had decided that with her fashion degree, she wanted to become a buyer. So she began researching potential companies to work for in order to get the training that she needed. To her surprise, one of the best companies to train with was the retail store she had left about eight months prior. She began to remember all the good things that she had liked about that particular company, which included the people with whom she had worked with.

Jenna realized that it definitely took her leaving that position for her to really appreciate what she had left behind. Even though it was the same company with some of the same employees, her perspective had now changed; it was again somewhere that she wanted to work. Jenna decided that she was going to make it her goal to go back to work for that department store and do whatever it took to get into the buyer program. She went into the store that night to talk with a current employee and friend. About two hours before she stopped in for a visit, one of the assistant floor managers up and quit. Perfect timing! This left an opportunity for her to get back into the company. She called and met with the general manager within the next couple of days. During this meeting, she explained that she would like to become a buyer, and she thought the company's training program would be a great place for her to start. He said that if she was serious, he would be more than happy to help her get into the buyer program because he thought she would definitely be an asset to the company. What a turn of events with Jenna's new perspective!

Here is another story about someone with whom I used to work. For the sake of the story, we will call him Tom. Tom was one of the happiest people I have ever seen; his happiness was contagious! We worked in an industry based on commissions and sales, but it did not seem to faze him even a little bit. He was never stressed out. He spoke to everyone like he was so genuinely happy to see them and hear their whole life story, if they wished to tell it. It was as if he did not have a care in the world, yet he had a family and two kids whom he was putting through college. He did not have a trust fund nor was he independently wealthy; he lived on a budget, like most people I know. You would think that he would have been a little more stressed out, living purely on a commission-based salary and putting two kids through college; but if he was, he never showed it. Time after time he would be one of the top sales people. I used to watch him to see if anything ever brought his spirits down. Broken sales deals, people running to a customer to make a sale, bad weather, rude customers, yet his attitude was always the same. He was just happy to be alive, proud of his kids and his family. He came to work with a smile on his face everyday. No matter how many hours he was at work, his smile never vanished! I watched day after day to see how long this could go on. Isn't that kind of sad in a way that the happiest guy in the workplace was the one who stood out the most over all others, as if it was fascinating? Happy people tend to stand out more than other people as they are less common. Grumpy people tend to be everywhere.

"Happiness is a gift from God that has been given to you. You can access it everyday, all day if you choose to and live your life in complete and total bliss! Or you can choose to save it and only bring it out for special occasions."

With Jenna, she changed her perspective on her job and that made a world of difference. Keep in mind that she was an active part in changing her perspective—she switched jobs. She did not just continue to work someplace where she was "incompatible" with, waiting for a change. She created change and therefore shifted her own perspective. Tom, on the other hand, had made a conscious choice everyday to choose happiness. I am sure that there was a day or two, now and then, when he was not, but for the most part his choice was obvious, even if you did not know him.

What is Soul Chemistry?

When there is a vibrational match between two or more people, it will raise everyone's vibration to create a new vibration, or a new harmony, and this is called Soul Chemistry. Our interaction with other people is a fascinating part of your Life Path. Our souls are designed to complement each other, as well as to help and learn from one another. When your vibrations are the same, and some of your abilities or interests are the same, each person is supported and uplifted by the other one's energy. When you find a vibrational match, something electrifying can happen. Imagine what it looks like when you put your hand on a static electricity ball and all of your hair stands on end. This is similar to what happens to you energetically when you find a vibrational match.

Soul Chemistry is kind of like this; imagine that you can hear one instrument playing music, and then another instrument is added, which alters the tone, and then another. Imagine that when these instruments begin to play, they complement each other in such a way that a beautiful song is created. This is what Soul Chemistry is like; the instruments can have a wonderful sound or tone all on their own, but they can also create a new beautiful song when played together. This music does not quite sound the same if it is played solo with just the one instrument. Soul Chemistry can be between two people in a romantic relationship or it can be between a group of people working together in the same field or in the same area of interest, having similar goals in mind. When a group of people works together with Soul Chemistry, great things can happen. Inventions are made, amazing music is written and played, and wonderful movies are filmed. Even huge movements in history have had the energetic power of Soul Chemistry. We all know when people have it, but most people never truly understand what it really is, let alone know how to find it for themselves.

Your Soul DNA is driven to seek out these matches. It is an internal drive to find vibrational matches in order to elevate one another, learn from one another and complement one's spiritual self. Your Soul DNA understands how to use Soul Chemistry to achieve optimal vibrational matches and create great things. It is most important for you to understand what Soul Chemistry is and try to utilize your Soul DNA knowledge. This will help you shift from what you think you are looking for, to seeking out matches for your highest good—in other words, to bring out the best in you. The mind and its logic is not usually thinking on the soul level, in fact it rarely is unless you have made a conscious decision to do so. Searching for Soul Chemistry and a good vibrational match takes on a whole different dynamic when you include free will. You choose your matches based on initial attraction or what you refer to as "chemistry" between you and another. Soul Chemistry is much deeper than an initial attraction. You have to get past the front cover (the physical self), and get to what is inside (the spiritual self), to see if there is Soul Chemistry.

Most people are no longer searching for vibrational matches to elevate one another, or to complement their soul and their spiritual self. They have lost touch with this part of their Soul DNA. But you do know that you are searching for something. When you are not paying attention to what is going on with your own vibration, you are definitely not paying any attention to what is going on with someone else's. It does not matter with whom you cross paths; energy is exchanged, and sometimes it can be good and other times it can be bad.

This energy will have an effect on your vibration, it can bring it up or it can bring it down. Let's talk about romantic relationships for a minute. You hear people talk about "soul mates" all of the time, finding their soul mate or being with their soul mate, as if it is one person. Usually you have many different soul mates and they can be here on earth or they can be on the Other Side. This is not the same as Soul Chemistry.

When you are not using your own gifts and internal knowledge to help you find a good match for yourself, you will end up spending way too much time trying to make a romantic relationship work that simply does not. On a daily basis people will spend more time and be more selective choosing something based on their wants and needs when they are picking out a car, a house, a pair of jeans or lunch for that matter, than they will spend picking out a potential partner.

Since most of the time, free will is involved when it comes to a romantic relationship, we do not listen to, or pay any attention to, the vibration and the energy of the other person. We tend to be overpowered by what you think is "chemistry" and blinded by what we think is love. We know that we are searching for something, and this must be it! When this happens it becomes harder and harder to view our relationship objectively. This will cause a problem, simply because we are not only dealing with the illusion of chemistry and love but our mind is now ruled by emotions. It takes time to get past the cover of a person to realize if he or she is a good match. This is when we get to know them on a deeper level. But by this time, we feel as if we have invested too much into the relationship to jump ship or that we are emotionally too attached to make the break if we are mismatched.

When you find Soul Chemistry on a deeper level it is very different. It is uplifting and things tend to flow very easily. It is not a chore and it is not draining. Soul Chemistry is empowering and brings out the best in you. When you find that with a husband, wife, boyfriend or girlfriend, you may be with that person for your entire life. When you do find a good match in your romantic life, you will still seek out more Soul Chemistry—only now it will be in the form of friendships.

When you are making bad choices, most of the time your friends will see past your whirlwind of emotions. They will usually state their opinion, which you will promptly throw out the window because, you think, they do not know what they are talking about; they are just jealous! But then you begin to wonder, why is it that so many relationships nowadays seem so complicated? Why can't I find the right person? Why am I so unhappy in this relationship?

Your Soul DNA is not meant to find someone to complete who you are; it is meant to find someone to complement who you are. You are already complete, and when you are desperately and blindly searching for someone, you most likely will not find what you are looking for. In other words when you are searching for someone with compatibility in mind, you are giving the Universe a mental picture of who you want to draw into your life. When you have no idea what you are looking for, but you are just desperate to be in a relationship, any kind of relationship, that is also what the Universe will send you.

> *"Why is it that most people will spend more time trying to decide what they want for lunch than deciding what qualities they would like in a potential partner? When it comes to lunch, people are very picky. They know what they like and what they don't like. When it comes to dating, they are like, "Whatever! They look cute!" Then they complain when the Universe sends them "Whatever"!*

If you are tired and worn out from your relationships in the past or in the present, try something different: choose your mate based on compatibility and Soul Chemistry. At least make yourself more aware of the Universal connection that you have with people and with your potential partners. When you open your eyes to the possibility that there might be another process to having and finding a good relationship, it makes you more aware of red flags that you otherwise would have ignored. It puts you more in tune with what your Soul DNA is looking for—someone who raises your vibration and complements who you are, and someone who is compatible with you and your needs. It will make you more aware of things that are important to you in a relationship, and it will shift your focus to at least determine if they have any of these qualities. It may draw to you people whom you may have over looked before.

> *"Imagine that all the women and men in the world are like puzzle pieces. When you are working on a puzzle, just because one puzzle piece does not fit, you do not throw it in the garbage and decide all of the puzzle pieces are the same. You know that they are all different, so you just keep looking until you find the perfect fit. Don't waste your time with the same puzzle piece, trying to make it fit. It will never work!"*

When your vibration matches another person's vibration, usually some of your abilities and interests are the same. When there is Soul Chemistry in a relationship, each person is supported and uplifted by the other one's energy. It is not draining, it is not hard, and it is most definitely not abusive or hurtful. Relationships based on Soul Chemistry absolutely exist. Some people just think that they are non-existent or are too good to be true because they have yet to experience one themselves. Most of the people who have not experienced this type of relationship have missed the opportunity because they are too busy making their non-compatible partner fit with them. They waste years of precious time and energy hoping that, one day, their relationship or their partner will become who they have always envisioned them to be. The sad thing is that most of the time people have an image in their head of who they want their partner to be, but that is not who they are at all. This is unfair to everyone involved.

> *"One of the biggest favors that you can do for yourself is to accept your loved ones for who they are and not be constantly disappointed because they are not who you think they should be."*

This is not uncommon at all; in fact, the opposite is true. People are terrified of being alone. Many will continue to stay in a bad relationship just to be with someone, anyone, even when they are not in harmony with the other person and his or her Soul DNA. When you stay in a bad situation or in an unhealthy relationship, your vibration goes way down. When that happens it does not only have a significant effect on your perspective but on your spiritual health as well. You must make an effort to change your perspective and/or move on.

> *"Why is it that you hold onto things that are not good for you, like a job or a relationship? It's because you already know what you have. If you let go you do not know what you are going to get. Why assume that if you make a change it could be worse? What if it is a million times better?"*

When you are in a bad relationship, it can feel as if you are in quicksand in the middle of an oasis. You want to stay right where you are, hoping that the quicksand will change to solid ground. You love where you are; it has all of these wonderful things, if only that one thing would change. That one thing seems to be a big thing, and you can feel yourself sinking, slowly but surely, deeper into the sand. You know that you need to either make a decision to get out now or you can wait, hoping that it will turn to solid ground and not engulf you completely. Maybe it will just stop when you are waist deep. So you stay, hoping that it will turn out the way you had hoped. You get deeper and deeper into the quicksand, and now it is making you nervous. The deeper you get the harder it becomes to move, and the harder it is to make your way out. Now you begin to panic, and you start to struggle a bit because you finally realize that it is what it always was, quicksand, with no bottom. It is nearly up to your chest now, and it is too late; major panic sets in and you need to get out. You really make an effort this time, but it is almost impossible. At this point one of two things can happen. You will manage to get out being completely exhausted and definitely scarred by what you just went through, or it will engulf you completely.

"If you are having a really hard time in your relationship, is it because you need to change your attitude or is it just time to move on? A lot of times people overlook the obvious because the fear of the unknown is terrifying!"

Soul Chemistry also exists among your family, your friends and your coworkers. Sometimes family and friends can be a wonderful vibrational match, and some of the time, they can be a terrible vibrational match. It is not uncommon for you to have had your vibration considerably lowered by family members or friends. When this happens you will feel it and notice it, but you won't know exactly why you feel this way. Sometimes family or friends leave you feeling terrible about yourself or they might be mean to you for no good reason. They might make rude comments to you, or maybe just have a negative outlook on life in general. To make it worse, when you have a bad vibrational match with your friends or your family, you usually believe that it must be tolerated. You may have been taught from a very young age that family is the most important thing. You may think that you must stay in contact with these people for the rest of your life. This is true when the family unit is uplifting and functional in a positive way. When the opposite is true, when your Souls are not in harmony, it can be very draining and awful.

Imagine hearing music playing again with one instrument, then adding another instrument and then another, just like before. But this time, instead of these instruments complementing each other with their different sounds, imagine what it would be like if they tried to play over each other and compete with one another. Imagine that each instrument is playing their own tune and trying to be as loud as they can because they want to be the only instrument that can be heard. Now it has become a competition and when that happens it creates chaos. The music is no longer soothing and beautiful; there is no harmony. There is just noise that sounds terrible and causes aggravation; then anger begins to set in. You can be dealing with the same instruments but experiencing a very different result. Chaos is quite powerful in its own right. But in the exact opposite direction of what your Soul DNA strives for. It is destructive and nonproductive to everyone involved.

When it comes to family, a lot of times you do not recognize what a bad vibrational match can do. Especially if you are not even aware of what Soul Chemistry is. You do know, however, that these family members make you upset or that you do not mesh well together.

"Some people mesh well together in relationships, friendships or families, and some people do not. Imagine that people are like ingredients; when mixed together they can either complement each other and make something amazing or create something horrible that is toxic to their system."

Communication can be tough. You can feel the negativity, and you do not know what to do about it. It is amazing how badly family and friends can sometimes treat each other and think that it is fine, that it is allowed. Some do not even think twice about it! Somehow they think that because they are your family or your friends that it gives them permission to misbehave or treat you worse than they would a complete stranger! Just because you are born into the same family, it absolutely does not give anyone the right to do this!

> *"Sometimes friends or family can be like weeds in a garden. Weeds compete for nutrients, water, sun and space. They rob the soil so much that it makes it hard for the healthy plants to grow. Remove anything from your garden that affects your ability to thrive and grow, let them fight and compete in someone else's garden."*

You will notice that when you are a bad vibrational match with someone, you tend to want to avoid these so-called family members or friends. This is your Soul DNA trying to remove you from anything having a negative effect on your well-being. It makes you want to protect yourself, such as keeping your distance, which you should. You can protect yourself by limiting your exposure or limiting contact with people who lower your vibration. However, when you do this, other people may judge your actions. This can make things even harder and even more complicated with friends or family. You have to remember to do what is best for you. Since everyone vibrates differently, you have to keep in mind that other people may have a very different relationship and experience with the person you are choosing to avoid. Some people will match vibrations with those whom you are a bad match with. If this is the case, they will have a hard time understanding your choice. We all have different vibrations, different perspectives and different past lives. This is all a part of our Soul DNA.

All you really need to do is simply recognize the different effects that people have on you and limit your time with people who have a less-than-positive effect. You can choose not to let them drain you or lower your vibration simply by being aware. You are in control, and you hold the key and the knowledge to live with people of all vibrations with great success!

> *"Different people have different effects on us since we are all energetic beings. Imagine people's energy as if they are rays from the sun. You can put on a hat and sunscreen, then go out and enjoy the day. Or you can go out, get burned, and be miserable for the rest of the week. You don't need to stay indoors; you just need to limit your exposure to the harmful rays!"*

Most people are usually blessed with more than one relationship that has wonderful Soul Chemistry whether the relationships are romantic, with family or with friends. Enjoy them and cherish them as they are a gift! Share knowledge, learn from them and teach them what you can. Spend time with them and feel the difference. Make this your gauge on what to strive for in your future relationships. Soul Chemistry can be abundant in your life if you just take time to keep your eyes peeled, recognize it and welcome it with open arms!

Your Energetic
Vibration

In the chapter about Soul Chemistry, you learned a little bit about individual vibrations and how someone else can affect you. Here I will go into a little more detail about vibrations and what it means to your physical existence and your spiritual being.

Your soul vibrates at many different levels, and several different things can affect your vibration. When your soul vibrates, an energy pattern is sent out by you and received by the Universe. Some animals communicate with each other through vibration in the different sounds they make. The human ear cannot always hear it, but a vibration is sent out and received in the form of communication. One thing that will have a direct impact on your vibration is when you are in harmony with the talents and abilities with which you have been gifted in your Soul DNA. When you are in tune with these gifts and pursuing your talents, your soul and spiritual being begin to vibrate at the perfect level. This allows you to have access to your Soul DNA information, and therefore, to become more in tune with the Universe and the Universal Laws. The Universal Laws can be a very complex subject to understand in the logical mind, but they are simplified and "understood" in the Soul DNA.

Everything in the Universe has a vibration to it. This is very important for you to understand. It is also important for you to be aware of your own vibration and when it is not in harmony with your Soul DNA. This happens when you are not following your own path to happiness or when you are around other people who are affecting your vibration in a negative way. You may think that this sounds a little complicated, but it is really not. This is something that you are born knowing, and you already notice it to some extent because it is in your Soul DNA.

One thing that is in constant vibration that you do notice, but probably do not pay much attention to, is the vibration of the planet earth. That is, of course, unless there is an earthquake, but this is not the type of vibration that we are talking about. The earth vibrates on an energetic level, as do the plants and the trees. However, different parts of the earth vibrate differently. So when you come to a city or a country that you love, and you cannot explain why you are so drawn to that particular area, it can have something to do with one of your past lives or it can have something to do with the vibration of that particular area. When you are in an area of the earth that vibrates well with your Soul DNA, the feeling is quite wonderful. Your mood is elevated and your health can feel better—you are in harmony with the Universe. Again, this can also be from living a past life in that particular area. But remember that knowledge and memories from past lives are also a part of what makes up your Soul DNA, thus creating harmony.

The following is an example of how people can be affected by different earth vibrations. I know two different people in the same family who suffered from anxiety. Anyone who knows about anxiety knows that it is a very difficult thing to deal with on a day-to-day basis. Because of financial and career reasons, the family decided to move from the area they had been living in for the better part of their lives to another state that was quite far away. When they moved an unexpected thing happened to two of the family members—their anxiety began to decrease drastically. Within months it seemed to have completely disappeared. One of the family members, Rachael, had been dealing with her anxiety issues for about twenty years. She had been through counseling for anxiety, she had read books, tried stress management and many different therapies, but nothing had worked. By the time she had moved, Rachael basically had learned how to manage and live with the anxiety to the best of her ability, assuming that she would have it forever. She had a hard time driving long distances alone, or going alone to an unfamiliar place. After the move, she started a new job and as a part of her new job she needed to drive quite far at least once a week to different meetings. Since she had just moved to the area, anywhere she needed to go would be unfamiliar territory to her and since it was for work she would be driving alone. Before the first couple of meetings, she began to prepare herself for the drive. Though she hoped the anxiety would not appear, she was pretty sure that it would have to be dealt with. The first meeting went really pretty well. Weird, she thought. It must be a fluke! Next week the meeting went even better. The next week was even better—the anxiety seemed to have completely vanished! It has been three years since the move, and still to this day, Rachael has experienced no anxiety. The new location is in harmony with her vibration.

The other family member, Joe, who was much younger, suffered from anxiety in crowded places and also did not like to drive. Just like Rachael, Joe expected no change with his anxiety and just assumed it would be a life long battle. He began going into some crowded places for different events and had minimal anxiety, which was very out of the ordinary for him. Then Joe began a new job and had to drive alone to different job sites. To his surprise he had no anxiety, nothing! This had never happened to him before, and it was a welcomed turn of events. To this day Joe is able to drive all over the place and go into crowded places anxiety free! Both Rachael and Joe were very skeptical that their anxiety would be gone for good, since it is common for anxiety to disappear and then with no warning suddenly return again. However, it has been three years with no return, and both of them are living an anxiety-free life!

That is a good example of how a different vibration in a particular area of the earth had an effect on two people's health in a way that caused them to no longer have anxiety; the new location was in harmony with their Soul DNA. A lot of times anxiety can also be caused by different energies as well as one's perception. The wonderful thing is that there is not just one place on earth that will offer a good vibrational match. The vibration of the earth differs throughout the globe. Thus there can be hundreds or thousands of places where you can live or to which you can travel where you will feel in harmony. This harmony can exist in different areas of the town in which you currently live. Your own vibration can also change over the years, many different times, depending on what is happening in your life. In other words, you may be a good vibrational match in one place and ten years later it is no longer a good match for you.

There are a lot of different things that can affect your vibration, and the earth is just one of them. You are affected by family members, coworkers and people with whom you are in relationships. The effect can be positive or it can be negative; the key is awareness. When you are around people in your life who are very draining, causing you harm or unhappiness, they will cause your vibration to lower. Just being around someone who has a negative attitude can even cause a temporary shift in your vibration. However, if you are aware of the effects that people have on your spiritual being, you can also make a choice not to let them affect you, simply by being aware and making that choice.

The reason that you want to pay attention to your vibration is because when your vibration is lowered, it affects a number of different things. Your mood is affected, your ability to tap into the Universal Laws is affected, it makes it harder to see things in a positive light and frustration sets in. Then you start doubting yourself, and with doubt usually comes the affirmation that you were right to doubt yourself in the first place. Since the Universe is attraction based and it does not have any attachment to your vibration or what you are energetically putting into it, your doubt is received and then it is returned. When your vibration lowers, you start to lose the connection between your spiritual body and your physical body, and therefore, your Soul DNA and its information. That knowledge begins to seem far away, very fast, and you cannot remember if you ever had any knowledge of the Universal Laws at all. This low vibration can take a toll on your physical health and cause you to have health issues. You feel as if you cannot remember how to come back into harmony with your spiritual being or how to raise your vibration again. You then begin searching for answers, starting from square one, trying to learn the basic spirit connection.

The opposite can also be true. Just being in the presence of someone who is in harmony with their Soul DNA can raise your vibration. When you have certain goals in life that you want to achieve or you have an interest in something, surrounding yourself with like-minded people can also raise your vibration. This not only raises your vibration, but it starts to change the energy pattern that you are sending out into the Universe. When you raise your vibration, your connection between your physical body and soul becomes stronger; they go hand in hand. This gives you more access to your Soul DNA knowledge and the ability to be in harmony with the Universe.

There is this woman whom I will call Christine. She was trying to begin a new career, which can be quite exhausting. She knew some people in the same industry, but none of them were in the field to the degree that she wanted to see herself. They were all very satisfied with being in the industry on a smaller scale, making enough money to get by, putting in just enough energy to get back what they needed. Christine had a different vision: of doing more, of being in the public more with several branches stemming from the same business. The people around her thought it sounded all right, but they were far from encouraging. As she began to develop her business and meet more people with the same thought process and goals, she began to do very well. They supported her ideas and they shared marketing strategies. They learned from each other's mistakes and successes. There was no competition, only support. This made quite a difference, not only in growing her new business but in their businesses as well. They referred clients to one another and shared business contacts. Slowly but surely, Christine's business began to take on the vision that she had imagined.

If Christine had continued to surround herself with her old acquaintances, who were not nearly as supportive, something very different may have happened. One major thing is that she may have begun to doubt her ability to achieve the level of success she desired. When you have people in your life telling you that something is not attainable or that you are not good enough for whatever it is that you want to achieve, you begin to question yourself. Those people are not in harmony with their Soul DNA, and therefore, they do not have access to the information that gives you endless possibilities! They do not even know that it exists. There are no limitations as far as the Universe goes—your dreams are limitless!

"Thinking is contagious ... so choose whom you surround yourself with carefully! Or at least take precautions so as not to infect yourself with other people's thinking!"

When you are with like-minded people you begin to visualize and brainstorm what it is you would like to accomplish. This is part of your Soul DNA; you have the knowledge of how to create things and how to attract into your life whatever it is you want. There is an energy that is created and it is very powerful!

Emotions and your perspective can also have a major impact on your vibration. You do have free will, and you all have different perspectives and different views, or the way you look at things. Is the glass half empty or half full? You know the saying. Well, some people have a positive attitude no matter what their situation is and for them the outcome is usually better. When you have a positive attitude and you look for the best outcome, your vibration raises. This energy pattern is then sent out into the Universe. With a high vibration and a message to the Universe, all things are in harmony. This takes us to the next chapter on the Law of Attraction.

"The Law of Attraction" Simplified

We use the Law of Attraction all day, every day without even realizing it. The Law of Attraction is one of the better-known Laws of the Universe because it has a magical feel to it. This is wonderful because it has finally become more of a focus for everyone, and it is finally being acknowledged. Many people seem to think that using the Law of Attraction entails a very concentrated effort; yet just as we eat, breathe and walk, our mind and bodies are involved with this Universal Law on an everyday basis, without being told. After all, it is a part of your spiritual knowledge and your Soul DNA.

When you realize that the Law of Attraction does indeed exist, you may think you need to do this: find a comfortable place, keep the kids quiet and have some time alone to begin creating your future. Yet as you sit in the room, you struggle to form a picture in your mind. You may become frustrated and try a few more times, but your mind starts wandering to the laundry and what you are making for dinner. "Wow, that was a chore! I'll try it again later in the week." Your mind fills with images of more laundry and grocery shopping. You think, this is a waste of time, forget about it, and go back to real life!

"When you are focusing on something in your life, it sends out energy waves of your thoughts. The Universe cannot tell the difference between if you want something to happen or if you do not, it just responds. So where is your focus?"

What you need to pay attention to are those thoughts that occur while you are driving in the car, waiting for a doctor's appointment, or lying in bed trying to fall asleep. This is usually when you are using the Law of Attraction, during these "zone-out" times. These are the times throughout the day when you are doing something on autopilot, which allows your mind to wander. As an adult you would be shocked to realize what it is that you spend most of your zone-out time thinking about, especially since you probably never really paid much attention to it up until now. More often than not, it is not about anything fun or exciting. It is usually about something that makes you feel a little bit more stressed out just by thinking about it. When you were a kid you would think about the new bike you wanted, where you would like to live when you grew up. This was because you had a close connection between your physical body and your Soul DNA, and you knew that anything was possible. Since you knew anything was possible, and you did not have any responsibilities that would sidetrack your mind, you spent your time daydreaming about fun things. Find the inner child in you and remember that soul/body connection. When you are driving to work, or when you are going to pick up the kids from school or soccer practice, use this precious time more wisely. Do not waste your zone-out time worrying about bills, the car or how you do not want to go to the grocery store.

Recently I went to get a safety check on my car. When they started checking the tires, I thought to myself, "It seems silly to check the tires. Wouldn't I notice if the tires were bad?" As I turned the steering wheel from one side to the other, the attendant said, "Ma'am, can you come and take a look at this?" So I got out of the car, thinking that he was going to point out that the tread on my tires was low, but I was shocked when he showed me what he had found. On both of the front tires, there were big chunks of rubber missing and the cable was exposed. I was very lucky that I had not blown out one of my front tires while driving. He informed me that I had to get the two front tires replaced to pass the safety check. I was more than happy to do this, but on the way to the tire store, I began to panic. I thought, "This is going to cost over a thousand dollars!" We had gotten a price quote for tires a little while back, and because the tires are a special size the quote was $2,400 for four tires! Then I started to think, "Where am I going to come up with an extra thousand dollars?" To make things worse, the only tire store I had found that carried the tire size I needed was in another town, and the tires were not in stock! All these thoughts were racing through my head as I was driving, and my stomach was getting tense. I finally realized what a turn my thoughts had taken all on their own, so I stopped myself and I changed my thoughts. I began to think: "What would make me feel better about this situation or at least less stressed out? What if I went to the local tire store and it happens to have the tires I need in stock?" Then I thought, "How about if they are on sale? How would that make me feel?" I started imagining that I had found the tires locally for a good price and how glad I was to get them replaced because, after all, this was a safety issue. This made me feel more relaxed and happy, so I decided to drive down to the local tire store and see what I could find. When I got to the store, to my surprise, they had indeed begun carrying the tire size that I needed, and they happened to have two left! Not only that, the tires were on sale! I ended up getting the two tires for such a good deal that my husband and I went back and bought the other two—all for under $800 total!

I couldn't believe it! I gave myself a pat on the back for stopping my gloom-and-doom attitude and for turning it into something positive.

When you find yourself doing this, you are sending mental pictures out into the Universe. The Universe has no attachment to what you are sending to it; it just responds. However, you need to understand that you can catch yourself and change the mental pictures you are sending out. The key is to actually catch yourself and consciously make the change. It can still be effective even if you do not start out on a positive note, as how it worked out for me with the tires. Pay more attention to the mental images that you are sending out into the Universe. Most of the time you are unaware of the effect you have on your own life, just from your thought process.

"Would you change your thoughts if you knew that they would become a reality? Just something to think about ..."

Here is a simplified plan:

1) Realize that you have a lot of "zone-out" time throughout the day. Any time of the day that you are on autopilot, you have a lot of time to think. When you are driving is a huge zone-out time, or right before you fall asleep, or when you are waiting for

your children or for scheduled appointments. All of these are huge zone-out times, times when you really want to catch yourself.

2) Use your "zone-out" time and replace it with "day-dreaming" time. Everyone is fond of daydreaming because it is a fun thing to do.

3) Daydreaming should consist of how you would love your life to be and what it would feel like to be living that life: being at a job you love, living in a different area of the city or the country, getting a new car, going on a vacation. It can be anything that makes you feel GOOD! There are no limitations in your daydreaming time. You are to create your dream exactly the way you want it.

4) The key to great daydreaming is that we allow ourselves to get lost in the feeling of being at a certain place in our life, or in the excitement of purchasing something that we have only "dreamed" about. This "feeling" is a big trigger for the Law of Attraction, much in the same way that panic is when we constantly feel as if we do not make enough money to cover the bills. That feeling will trigger the Law of Attraction to manifest into an unfavorable outcome, because the feeling is intense and believable. So it is really important to make a conscious effort to "feel good" about something with the same intensity and that can happen when we daydream.

5) If you have worries that creep into your mind, replace the worry with a scenario in your head of how you would like it to be resolved. Because problems do pop up, you should adopt a new policy: that when a problem arises a solution will shortly follow. Only solutions are allowed in your "zone-out" time. Remember, this is daydream time, so do not question if this is going to work. Just lose yourself in the feeling of being stress free and in the great feeling of the daydreaming itself.

6) It is very important to recognize and acknowledge what you have created in the past and for the future. When you use your zone-out time for good and create the outcome that you want, take a moment to acknowledge what a good job you did. Each time you take a small moment to be proud of how you solved a problem, it will give you more and more control over the Law of Attraction in your life.

When you recognize and acknowledge what you did do and notice that you did have an effect on the outcome, it becomes easier to do. You begin to understand the correlation between your mental pictures and the events that take place in your life. You begin to understand how your mental pictures can create the exact opposite of what you want to bring into your life. Your involvement and the role you play when working with the Law of Attraction begins to make more sense. When you begin to connect the dots, it will give you a better idea of how to work with this law more effectively.

People waste way too much precious daydreaming time on everyday issues, which get handled whether we think about them while driving or not. Let's face it—dinner will still get made, laundry will still get done, and the car will still get fixed. So, if you replace this time with daydreaming time, you will be a much happier person; you will notice that your mood will be lighter, and you will begin to attract more positive things into your life. Moods are contagious, so your family and coworkers will thank you for this. Life will feel easier because in your daydreaming time life is more enjoyable and everyday tasks are not such a chore. Also, problems that do arise will be solved much quicker and will not feel as hard to conquer.

Most people review their problems as least five times a day instead of using this time for daydreaming. You can learn something from all of those smiling kids who want to know, "Why can't I go into space? They have the space shuttle, don't they?" If you think about it, someone has to go into space, purchase the vacation or buy the new car; so why not you? What do you have to lose! I love the saying, "If you are going to be thinking anyway, you might as well think big!"

Intuition & Psychic Ability

Intuition and psychic ability is something that is very much a part of your Soul DNA. You are born with this ability. Everyone has this ability. It is truly your sixth sense. Most of the time, you will not pay much attention to your own intuition until you go against it, and then you will say to yourself, "I knew I shouldn't have done that! I just had a feeling!" Intuition is just that, when you have "a feeling" about something, something that you should or shouldn't do; again this feeling is usually felt in the body. Most of the time you will refer to it as your "gut" feeling. Your intuition or your gut feeling, is your psychic ability, and you are tapping into all of your resources to get information that is needed at that time.

Most children are born with a clear memory of their spiritual being and of the Other Side. Children know that being able to hear or see things, such as their Spirit Guides, and being able to use their own intuition or psychic abilities is part of their Soul DNA. It is just natural for them to use these abilities; and since they still have a strong memory of the Other Side, that is what they think that they are supposed to be doing. These abilities are a part of the tools that we have been given, and the tools are there to be utilized.

> *"You are given a manual (intuition) to help guide you. But, instead of using it, people go about life the hard way. It's like buying something unassembled and promptly throwing out the instructions (because that is what everyone else does), then getting frustrated because you are having trouble putting it together."*

As you get older, you become exposed to all kinds of people who have shed any memory of the Other Side, their Soul DNA and their own intuition. These people have developed a different mindset that does not include using all of their spiritual tools. Many times parents will teach their children limitations in the real world; they will try to bring them more into the physical realm and what the parents believe is reality. So children begin to lose the memory of their intuition and start to question what they thought they knew. After all, our parents, our teachers and our mentors are adults! They must know what they are talking about.

When you are a child and you are surrounded by people who question your abilities and what it is that you are seeing or hearing, it can make you very scared. Since it also scares the parents, who have usually forgotten all about their own abilities, they do not know what else to do but tell that child it is his or her imagination. Because to them it *is* the child's imagination—a child cannot possibly "know" things or "hear" things that he or she cannot physically see. As a parent or a caregiver, when you have a child around you experiencing these things, it may bring up memories from when you were a child and remind you of the experiences that you had.

I do want to point out that just because you are psychic when you are born does not necessarily mean that you will become a professional psychic when you get older. Not everyone who can play a sport will turn professional; but sports are wonderful for your health, and they should always be a part of your life. I have been psychic and a Spiritual Teacher in many, many of my past lives as well as this one. This is very much a part of my abilities and a part of what makes up my own Soul DNA. I have two children who are also psychic but they are not meant to take the same life path as me; they have different talents, abilities and careers ahead of them.

Here is a story about my own children and me. While watching a show on television about psychic children, I thought back to my own childhood and remembered how frightening it could be. Since I have had a strong psychic ability my whole life, I never grew up knowing what it is like to be what people call "normal." I grew up naturally thinking that everyone was like me. It wasn't until I got older that I realized that not everyone had the same abilities as I did, and I was a little confused. Since birth one of my many psychic abilities has been claircognizance—I would just "know" things. People would say, "How do you just know? You can't just know!" Well, you see, I thought everyone just knew things, so I thought it was weird that they didn't "know" what I was talking about. I wondered why they weren't tapping into their own gifts and abilities. As I grew older, I realized that I was indeed very different. People did not understand what I was seeing, hearing or what I was trying to explain. It became frustrating for me so I just stopped talking to them about it.

When I became a teenager, I became really skeptical. This is a very natural occurrence. If you haven't tried to block your abilities before your teenage years, this is usually the time it happens. After much skepticism from friends and adults, I started to question my own abilities. I began to wonder, "How do I just know things? Other people don't just know things. How do I? What makes me different? How do I know that I am even right?" So I decided to pretend that I was no longer psychic, easy as that! Well, it's not so easy. One morning while I was sitting in class I had a vision about me being in a car wreck after school that day and had a very strong "feeling" that I should go home early. I thought, whatever, I will just ignore it and it will go away. Until now I usually followed my feelings because I thought they were a part of my guidance system, my Soul DNA. Since this had been the case up until that day, everything had always worked out fine. But this particular day, I decided to no longer "know" things. I was determined, so I shut out all of the thoughts for the rest of the day and ignored them. I had done a really good job and had even forgotten about it by the time I was leaving school with a friend. I was about three blocks away when we got into a four-car accident. That was when I realized that ignoring "knowing" things did not work for me. That was a huge lesson! Though my friend and I only had minor injuries, it was the last time I decided to "challenge" my own abilities.

Now, "coming out of the closet" as a psychic was not easy either. People did not and still do not always believe that I have the gifts and abilities that I have. They do not even stop to think that they have some of the same abilities! That is really interesting to me because I do not think that I have ever met anyone who has not had his or her own "gut" feeling about something, at least once. For me, however, this is my path, and I accept being this way. It is a way of life for me, not something that I do for fun.

For my own children, it was very different. Since I was already a psychic, my understanding of their gift and my ability to explain to them what it was they were seeing and hearing was very helpful. From the time that he was very young, my son would see spirits all over the place. I remember driving by an empty lot one day, where certain people I knew had asked me if they should put up a business there. I had told them to look elsewhere, that the vibration and energy were not good on that lot and it would affect any business that opened up there. While driving by the empty lot I asked my son, "What do you see over there?" He said, "A man in a robe, right there. Oh no, you can't see him anymore. He ran behind that church!" "What church?" I asked. He looked back and could no longer see the church. His eyes grew really big, and he asked, "The church is gone! Why did I see that?" I told him that he was seeing an old church that was on that piece of property years ago, and the monk was in the same time frame as the church. He then added he did not like that area, that it felt weird. His observations were correct. There was an energy imprint on that piece of property, and a lot of strange things had happened there over the years, which has not helped to improve the area.

My kids have grown up knowing that the spirits they see are real, and there is nothing for them to be scared of for they cannot hurt them in any way. We are spiritual beings. We have always had a lot of spirits around and about the homes in which we have lived. My kids and

I always talked about the spirits that are in our houses, even the mischievous ones. This helped my children to understand that they are a part of life. When my son was little, he used to say, "I feel sorry for people who do not have spirits around. It must feel lonely." I agree … I like feeling them around too.

Knowledge is very important. If you do not know the answers to your children's questions, buy a book or talk with someone who might know the answer. Let them know that all of their questions are good ones. For you and your children, knowledge is power!

If you are no longer a child and you are wondering as to how or if you can get your abilities back, know that this is a wonderful question—and yes you can! It begins with simply realizing and acknowledging that you and everyone else on the planet has intuition and psychic abilities, and it is a part of your Soul DNA makeup. It is a gift that is meant to be used, and it can be very helpful with your life path and with your journey. You do not lose this ability. It just needs to be remembered and used again. The more you use it, the easier it becomes to access. Trust is the next thing because at first you may question yourself. How do you know if what you are thinking or feeling is real or something that you made up in your mind? One of the things that I love to teach people, and something that I use myself, is intuitive decision making. It is a very simple thing to do, and it is very accurate. Your intuition is felt in your heart center, not your head. If you need help in making a decision, all you need to think of is whatever it is that you would like answered and pay attention to how it feels in the heart center. Does it feel right and good or wrong and weird? Your question can be anything from, "Should I buy this car?" to "Is this route the fastest way home?" Do not second-guess this information. This is a good way to practice and tap into your intuition.

"When you are having a difficult time making a decision, try using your heart center instead of forcing yourself to think through it. You will know that it is a good decision if in your heart it feels right. Sometimes your head has ulterior motives!"

A lot of people think that intuition is something that you know in your head, but it is actually more in the body. When you begin to get more in tune with your body's senses and your intuition, you can then learn to separate them from the thoughts that creep into your head. This does take practice; but the more you practice, the easier it becomes. When you are only using your mind and its logic, all kinds of things can interfere such as ego, judgment, etcetera. You hear things that other people have said and you think about other people's reactions; this is not spirit based. When you are tapping into your intuition and your heart center, you are also tapping into a web of knowledge that is spirit based.

Tips for helping Intuitive Children:

Here are some easy things that I put together to help you with psychic children. My son and daughter are very well-adjusted kids. They do not live in fear of their abilities; they live in harmony with them. This information can help intuitive children live basically "normal" lives without fear:

1) Realize that because your child is psychic, it does not mean that he or she is meant to become a psychic, do readings, etcetera. This is not the path that my children will take.

2) It is important to make sure that your children understand what their ability is. It is good for them to know if they are an empath, what an empath is, etcetera. Also, their gifts and abilities are real and will most likely always be a part of their everyday life. You want to teach them how to live in harmony with their abilities and to be comfortable with them. However, in time they can learn, to some extent, how to tune it out.

3) Make sure that your children know that spirits will not harm them! It is hard for psychics and intuitives to sleep at night without hearing all kinds of spiritual racket. Keeping the television on helped my son to sleep. I do this myself most nights; it drowns out the

noise and gives my mind something else to listen to. Spirits are active at night, and our minds are very receptive when we are going to sleep. It is like opening the floodgates to the Other Side.

4) Being psychic can be energetically draining. Your children should learn psychic protection if they need to. If they are not paying attention, they pick up on other people's energy and take on their emotions without realizing it. This can happen anywhere, especially in a crowded area such as a mall or at school. If this is a problem have them imagine themselves in a bubble surrounded by a white light that does not allow another's energy to get through. Then have them ask God to dissolve other people's energy into the white light of the Holy Spirit. Have them do this before you go somewhere crowded. Taking on everyone else's feelings can make you feel anxious, especially somewhere like a department store. You can also just choose not to be affected by this. If you recognize that these feelings are not your own, you can tell your body that you are calm and healthy. Decide that you will not allow another person's emotions to make you feel any differently. You have control over your own body!

5) It is also important to pay attention to what your children say and to take them seriously; do not disregard what they are saying because they are young.

For instance, if they do not like someone or they are uncomfortable with a specific situation, there is usually a very valid reason. Children can sense someone's energy and intentions like nobody's business.

6) You need to let your children know that they are in total control. Sometimes when you are in tune with your psychic abilities, there is a feeling of having no control over what you are experiencing. You can ask not to be shown things that you cannot do anything about or that you have no control over. For instance, it was very scary when I was younger and knew that my little brother was going to be in a car accident. I had no control over this; and I just had to wait and pray that he would be okay. Luckily, as he drove his car off of a ravine, it happened to land on the only pile of trees in that area. This barely kept his car from launching over the hill several hundred feet to the bottom. I asked not to be shown these things that I have no control over, and have not had this sort of problem since.

7) Decide if and when to let others know about their abilities. I did discuss with my children that their friends and the parents of their friends may have a hard time understanding their gifts. I left it up to them to let their friends know about their abilities or mine. Remember, your child is psychic; you need to trust his or her judgment.

Consciousness Web

Within your Soul DNA is also a connection to what is called a Consciousness Web. A Consciousness Web is a spiritual communication system and a web of knowledge. My Spirit Guides tell me that this Consciousness Web is a little hard for our logical mind to understand. They explained to me that this web of knowledge is similar to how millions of atoms can make up one particular thing, like a basketball. The difference is, instead of being separate, it would be as if all of the millions of atoms had a tiny string that connects each and every one of them together like a web. The basketball would be the Consciousness Web, and the atoms would be each and every one of us. This is one of the Universal Laws in fact. "The Law of One or Oneness," our spiritual being is all a part of a bigger whole, or in this case, the Consciousness Web. We can still move about freely but there is still that little string of energy that connects all of us together.

Since we are all on the same web, or communication system, this allows us to receive telepathic information from spirits or our Spirit Guides. They can send images or pictures to us, which are received as thoughts or words and may have a lot of valuable information. It is a communication system to which everyone has access. Different books are written by accessing this Consciousness Web and its information. It is also a way that psychics and mediums get an abundance of information. We can tap into this web of knowledge to get information about the Universal Laws, solving a problem, health issues or whatever we wish.

Most of the time when we are accessing this web of knowledge, we do not even realize that we are doing it. Primarily we will access it when we are sleeping because we tend to be more receptive to whatever information is coming through to us at this time. When we are sleeping, our spiritual being will connect into this web of knowledge without any interference from the mind and its logic. This is why many people who do not consider themselves psychic can have a premonition dream that comes true. They just tap into whatever information is going through the Consciousness Web at that time. Sometimes when a major event is about to happen, that information will be going out in many areas of the web at the same time. This allows many people to have the same premonitions about a major change or event while they are sleeping.

You can have a little more control over the information that you receive if you choose to. You can go to bed asking for an answer about something, and if you wake up with the answer that you were looking for, this means that your spiritual being tapped into that web of knowledge until the specific answer was found. Since you naturally access the Consciousness Web several times a week, this is also a great time for loved ones who have released their physical body or your Spirit Guides to communicate with you. It is a wonderful communication tool.

I do this a lot when I am searching for information about something, especially spiritually based information. I will go to sleep and find myself having access to all kinds of information and then waking up with the answers that I am looking for. In my case I have been aware of what it is that I am doing for so long that I will usually have a clear memory of it when I awaken. It is similar to downloading something onto a computer. Many great writers have acquired information for novels or movies this way; many psychics receive predictions this way. People have even found cures for diseases. It can be like a Universal Library if you know how to access it.

On a more advanced level, the Consciousness Web can be accessed in a meditative state. Many Buddhist monks practice this for years and have acquired knowledge far beyond what is usually tapped into. There are stories of Buddhist monks, after years of practice, being able to levitate and transport themselves from one place to another. There are tales of yogis being able to control their bodies and to slow their hearts down so much so that they do not have a pulse. These are very good examples of the kind of knowledge that can be attained through the Consciousness Web.

Another wonderful bit of information that you can have access to on this web of knowledge is the Universal Laws. It is here where all of the information about the Universal Laws is accessed. Try using your pass to the Universal Library. There are no fees, it has information on everything, and you are a lifetime member!

Past Lives and Past Life Memories

This is a fun subject for most everyone. People have wonderful ideas of who they were in their past lives. What people do not think about is that past lives often do have an impact on who you are in this lifetime. The memories that you carry over from past lives, whether they are of fear or happiness, are all stored in the same place, in your Soul DNA memory bank. You have a collection of experiences blended together from all of your lifetimes. It can be very wonderful and confusing at the same time.

Many people wonder about their past lives, usually someone will have an idea of who they were or where they lived. Now keep in mind that the chances of you being a famous king or queen is probably about as likely as you being someone famous in this lifetime; and truth be told, it is really not that important. You have lived many wonderful past lives in different areas of the world and many not so wonderful. Throughout all of your lifetimes you have encountered many, many people. Take everyone that you know in this lifetime, for instance, and multiply that number times thirty—now that is a lot of people! That does not mean that everyone has had thirty past lives; the amount of past lives that people have lived varies. What is important is how the experiences you have had in those past lives affects your life today. How can this affect your life today, you wonder? Well, it plays into your current life in many different ways. For example have you ever felt a strong tie to a place or country that you have never been to before? It can be somewhere foreign or somewhere close to home. Usually you will have a strong desire to go to that place. It is almost like a longing, only you do not understand why. It is just somewhere that has always fascinated you. You can even have this feeling come over you from looking at a photograph. Sometimes people will travel to foreign places and say that it felt like home to them. That is really an amazing experience.

My daughter is completely fascinated with Paris, France; she has been since she was very young. She always decorated her room with pictures of the Eiffel Tower and other

Parisian type decor. This is because she has lived a very wonderful past life there. One time when she was doing a past life regression she went back to that lifetime and the place that she had lived. A wonderful feeling came over her and it became very clear that in that past life she was very happy. She could see the Eiffel Tower from the window of her home.

On the flip side of that, she also lived during the Holocaust. During middle school they had to read a book about the Holocaust, and this opened up another door for her. She began to have dreams about where she was and the things that were happening around her. She was a young woman who had a small child, and they became separated. This was not a wonderful life for her at all, and there were many nights of lost sleep from those horrible memories. We would all talk about it. She knew that she was remembering a past life, so she would ask to release it when she went to bed. Instead of having the reaction that a lot of people would, she had the opposite. She studied more and more about the Holocaust and learned as much as she could about what went on at that time. It helped her to understand what she was seeing in her dreams. She became more educated on the subject; then after awhile, the dreams disappeared. If this happens to you, you can ask God to release the memory from your Soul DNA and just remind yourself that you are very safe in this lifetime. Even though it can be unpleasant, by making that decision, you can decide not to let it interfere with your life now.

There are other things that are not so much fun that can be tied to past lives, such as the fear of drowning. I have a family member that has a memory of drowning in a past life so water scares her. Fears of this nature can sometimes be overwhelming. The reason for this is that usually the person with the fear of water or bridges or whatever it may be does not recognize that the fear is from a past life. Especially if they have no memory of that past life, they somehow think that it is a valid fear from this lifetime. The way that you can usually tell the difference is if you have not had any bad experiences that you or your parents can remember that would have caused your fear of water, etcetera. It is usually from a past life. Past life regression and hypnosis sometimes can be helpful for you to remember those past lives and help you to release them.

Sometimes you may have an interest or the drive to learn more on a subject without knowing why. It is very common for you to do many of the same things throughout several different lifetimes since you have the same gifts and abilities in your Soul DNA and, therefore, in each lifetime. For instance, I have been a psychic and

Spiritual Teacher in many, many of my past lives. It is definitely a theme with me. My dad has been a musician in many of his past lives, and my son, an athlete.

You may also know or meet people who you have shared past lives with. Have you ever met someone for the first time and felt an instant connection with them, as if you have known them forever? This is because it resonates with your Soul DNA and your memory of them. This can be with a friend or with a romantic partner. With friends this does not seem to be a problem; you become fast friends and usually stay that way.

On the other hand, if it is with a romantic partner, it can sometimes be different. Sometimes the relationship does not work out, yet people still feel very drawn to that particular person and they cannot understand why. They try to pursue the relationship even though they know that it is not a very good fit for them. Something is pulling them to that person and they just cannot explain it. When I have done past life readings for people in this situation, when they realize that it is only a past life memory and that they are retaining unresolved feelings from another lifetime, it seems to help them release the connection and move on. Most of the time when they are told that it was a past life connection, their reaction is, "I knew it!" Deep down on a spiritual level this makes sense to them; it makes sense in the heart center.

Children can have very strong past life memories of people they know or places they have been since they have only recently come from the Other Side. Let's take my son, for example. I remember that when he was four, he asked me if he could have some ice cream. I said, "Sure!" He said to me, "You are the best mom ever, much better than my last mom." He continued, "But she was only my mom in one lifetime, and you have been my mom in four lifetimes. My dad was not the same dad that I have in this lifetime. He was a different dad. He used to chop wood, a lot!" What a wonderful experience to hear him talk so clearly about his past lives. Children can have very clear past life memories, and it is really interesting to ask them about it. It is not harmful in any way, and they usually really enjoy telling you their story. I have heard some really fun stories about children who remembered being grandparents to family members. Sometimes they can remember a location or place without ever having been there before. It is in their Soul DNA memory bank. Although my son does not really remember this anymore, we still talk about it and laugh. It makes for a great story!

Releasing Your Physical Body

At the end of your time here on earth, your spiritual body and your physical body will separate. You will release your physical body and go back to living in the spiritual realm. This does not mean that you cease to exist; this means that your physical body ceases to exist. Your spiritual body and the essence of who you are will continue to be very much alive on the Other Side. You will meet up with people whom you have not spent time with in a while. They will be people whom you know from your journey here on earth and some of them you know from the Other Side. You work, you socialize, you teach and learn—you name it, life goes on!

Your physical existence is not who you are. You are a spiritual being. The very essence of who you are is in your Soul DNA and that exists in your spiritual body. You are only in your physical body for a short period of time. Many seem to think that it is the other way around. Many people believe that we are a physical being first and then somehow we become a spirit when our time here on earth is done. Some people even believe that when we are no longer in our physical body, we just cease to exist entirely.

Throughout my life I have been able to hear spirits and see them. They have always been very much a part of my life. I sense them around me all of the time. So when someone releases their physical body, I never, ever have the feeling that they just cease to exist. As far as I am concerned, they have simply moved on to a different realm. They will continue to visit and continue to communicate; it was just not in the physical realm. One day I thought about what it would be like to believe that when you crossed over, that you just cease to exist. That would mean that if a loved one died you would never, ever hear from them or see them again. For people who believe this, it has to be some of the most unbearable pain imaginable! It would absolutely be a miracle, if you ask me, for some people to ever heal from that kind of pain.

This became very real to me when I was giving a reading to someone who was having a really hard time moving on when one of her loved ones had crossed over. This poor woman was so overcome with grief. During my talk with her, I realized that she was trying to expand her knowledge on what happens when you release your physical body. Until this time she had spent most of her life thinking that when you crossed over that was it. You were just gone, forever!

What happens when you release your physical body is that you go into an orientation. This is to help you adjust back into the spiritual realm. Sometimes your release can be rather quick or unexpected, so if this happens, it is important to regroup. You also go into an area where you reflect on all that you have learned and how your time was spent while you were on your journey here on earth. After this orientation, it is back to your normal state of existence.

You may come and see your loved ones that are still in the physical realm. Sometimes communication can be difficult, especially if your loved ones do not fully understand their own existence. If they are not in touch with their spiritual being and their Soul DNA, it makes communication a little more difficult. You will see things from a very different perspective, and you will understand all of the different lessons that your loved ones are going through. You will not hold any anger or resentment, or judge anyone for their actions. When you are in your natural state of existence, you only come from a place of love.

If you have had a loved one who has released their physical body and you do not feel them around, this does not mean that they are not around you. They are usually very much around you. When you are really grounded in the physical world and your physical existence, and you are not in tune with your spiritual body or your Soul DNA, your spiritual senses are more desensitized. In other words your sensitivity to messages from your loved ones or your ability to sense them around you is really dull. You can be grounded in your physical body and still have a good connection with your spiritual body. In fact this is very important; it creates balance.

If you are too grounded in your physical existence, sensing a loved one can be like this. Imagine being blindfolded, trying to feel if someone is lightly touching your foot … through your shoe. If they are just touching the shoe, you most likely will not feel it. If you remove the shoe and someone touches your foot lightly, you will definitely feel it. You will feel it because they are touching your skin, and because you are using all of your senses, the shoe is not blocking the sensation. Your senses are very aware of what is happening. If you are not sensing your loved one around, you probably need to remove the shoe, or whatever is blocking your sensitivity.

Usually over time, by simply learning and practicing many of the things that you have learned so far, and by understanding what your true existence is—that your physical body only plays a temporary role in your life—you can learn to heighten your spiritual senses. You need to pay more attention to all of your senses, most importantly your spiritual senses. Those are the ones that are felt in the body and in the heart center. When you understand more about your creation, who you are, your spiritual body and your Soul DNA, things will change dramatically for you. You will feel better, and you will have endless possibilities and endless potential. You will feel a stronger connection to your Spirit Guides and to your loved ones who are no longer a part of the physical realm. Life will become more enjoyable and goals will become easier to achieve!

"Enjoy your journey here on earth. Everyone has their own special journey and it is one to be cherished!"

Universal Prayer

May I always see the signs that you send me.

May I always remember to follow my passion.

May I always understand that possibilities are endless.

May I always choose happiness.

May I always live knowing there is plenty to go around.

May I always feel the abundance of the Universe.

May I always know this is an attraction based Universe.

May I always enjoy every day and say to you, "Thank you for all that you provide!"

~ Jennifer O'Neill

KEYS to the SPIRIT WORLD

An Easy To Use Handbook For Contacting Your Spirit Guides

Jennifer O'Neill

What Is A Spirit Guide?

Many people have heard of Spirit Guides, however, a lot of people are left wondering, "What exactly is a Spirit Guide?" This is a really great question and I am happy to answer it. But in order to answer this question, I would like to start out by giving you a little bit more information, or knowledge, on your creation as a spiritual being.

When all spirits were created, you (as a spirit) were created with the ability to incarnate here on earth. In other words, you have the unique ability to exist not only in the spiritual realm, in your natural state of existence, but in the physical realm as well. Amazing! So you were created with the ability to live as many lifetimes as you wish here in the physical realm, in order to learn and grow spiritually to the best of your ability. You choose when to incarnate here on earth, as well as how many lifetimes you would like to experience. This allows you to gain knowledge that is only possible for you to obtain by living many lifetimes in the physical realm, by being a human being, not just a spiritual being.

With this wonderful ability certain precautions, or safeguards, were put into place to make sure that you get the most possible spiritual growth out of each reincarnation. What is reincarnation? The same as incarnation; choosing to be born into the physical world in order to learn and grow spiritually from the encounters you have here on earth, throughout each lifetime. One of the safeguards put into place for your trip into the physical realm was to make sure that you never make this transition alone, or without any spiritual guidance from the "Other Side." Why? Well, because it makes good sense. Just think about it; you are a spiritual being having a physical experience, not the other way around. When you adapt into the physical realm, there are a lot of adjustments that need to be made. During this transition you can also get what I call "spiritual amnesia." What is spiritual amnesia? It's when you forget about the spiritual realm, and your natural state of existence. Why should it matter if you forget about the spiritual realm, why you are here on earth, while in the physical realm? Because, if this happens, you also forget about the many spiritual tools that you have access to. These tools, in actuality, work very well in the physical realm. However, it is hard to access something that you have forgotten about. There are many things that you are capable of, things that are not taught to you when you are in physical form. In fact, you when you are in physical form, most people are taught how *not* to use their spiritual tools. It is for these reasons mentioned, that you are required to have some form of spiritual guidance.

Spiritual guidance comes to you through different avenues, and in different forms. One important avenue is by the way of a Spirit Guide. Spirit Guides are regular spirits, just like you, who have incarnated here on earth at least one time before. These spirits make a choice, or choose, to become a Spirit Guide to other spirits. It is something that they wish to do, like a career path. When a spirit chooses Spirit Guide as a path they wish to pursue, they are required to go through a training process in which they are specially taught to do the job. The preparation is thorough and intense (since their job requires dealing with the hard headedness we have become so accustomed to when we get here).

So when you choose to reincarnate on earth, one of the things that is essential before you make the trip, is to choose a trained Spirit Guide. This Spirit Guide will then help you to get things in order for your up and coming journey. They will help you most importantly to create your life path or your chart. Your life path or chart is a spiritual blueprint of your physical life, mapping out your journey. How does this happen? You and your Spirit Guide will map out your chart together, by giving serious thought to all of the things that you would like to experience and accomplish while you are here on earth, in the physical realm. This allows your Spirit Guide to have a very clear vision of what you are trying to accomplish from your own perspective. They have, in fact, helped you to create the very path that you are on now!

When you incarnate, and you are no longer on the "Other Side" (you are now on the physical plane), your Spirit Guide's job is to look after you. They help to guide you according to the plan, or life path, that you designed for yourself, together on the "Other Side." They try their best to keep you "on track" so to speak. They help to give you courage, strength, and knowledge, all the while watching out for your charts. However, they have other jobs too. Those jobs also include recruiting other specialized guides or Angels if needed, as well as helping you with spiritual or energetic protection. All with the same purpose, to help you achieve the things that you are here to achieve, in accordance with your chart. If you get way off track, which is common, your Spirit Guide will do whatever they can to steer you back in the right direction.

Spirit Guides cannot be anyone that you know from this lifetime. Because that would mean at some point, while you were here on earth, you were without any spiritual guidance, and that simply cannot happen. In other words, just to make it clear, your Spirit Guide is not your grandmother, dad, sister, or friend from this lifetime. You cannot have been alive at the same time, during this lifetime, as your current Spirit Guide. They can be, however, someone that you were close to in another lifetime, like a friend or relative from a past life or different lifetime. In fact, that is very common!

Although you have one main Spirit Guide, you can have other Spirit Guides join you throughout your lifetime journey. The one that I have been talking about up until this point is your main Spirit Guide, or your general Spirit Guide. The Spirit Guide who stays with you always, from birth, until you leave this physical plane. However, you can also have other specialized Spirit Guides that come into your life and stay with you for a shorter period of time. They can be with you for a long or a short duration depending on what is necessary or happening in your life at the time. These specialized Spirit Guides come in at different times of your life in order to help teach you about something that you are trying to learn, or help you with a skill that you are trying to develop. Things such as Reiki, healing, cooking, sports, health, etcetera, may require a different type of Spiritual Guide. They can also come in during periods of hardship, like if you are battling an addiction or having a health issue. During this time, your general Spirit Guide is still working in your corner, on your behalf, as your main Spirit Guide. When other specialized Spirit Guides are called in, they all work together as a team. One does not bow out so that another one can take its place. In fact, like I mentioned before, your general Spirit Guide is usually the one who recruits other specialized guides in the first place, in order to help you and give you further guidance. There is no competition among Spirit Guides, they all have the utmost respect for each other, and have your best interest at heart. They come from a place of guidance and love.

Besides recruiting specialized Spirit Guides to help you in time of need, your general Spirit Guide's job is to also, as I mentioned before, work with your Angels. There are many different types of Angels on the "Other Side" (which is a whole different book), so when your Spirit Guide sees that you are in need (if you have not asked for them already), they will recruit or call in Angels. They know which Angels to call upon and how many to bring in. Just like Spirit Guides, Angels have different jobs, according to their phylum, so it is helpful that your Spirit Guide knows which ones to call upon. Your guide can also go to the higher phylum of Angels in order to request help to intervene with your chart if necessary. Spirit Guides do not have the authority to intervene with your charts, but Angels do. This might happen if you have strayed so far off your path that your chart may actually need to be altered. Getting off of your path this far usually happens because we exercise free will and stubbornness. Many times when people get frustrated and think that they have no spiritual guidance, it's not because they do not have any, it's because they have the right to ignore their Spirit Guides. Free will is very powerful! You have the right and ability to go against your own spiritual wishes or desires, which many people do a really good job of doing. Especially when they think what they really want differs on the physical plain from what they had originally intended when they were in the spiritual realm. When you get too far away, or disconnected, from who you are on a soul level, you can be enticed in other directions causing you to head down a dangerous or destructive road. That would be an instance when your Spirit Guide may have to take measures into their own hands and have your chart altered.

Your Spirit Guides are your protectors. As a spiritual being yourself, it is important that you have spiritual support, even if you choose to ignore it. However, if you are reading this book, most likely you have not chosen to ignore your Spirit Guides at all. Up until this point, you have probably just not had all of the knowledge required to advance your spirit communication skills and allow you to truly understand the entire process. In order to be successful, it is important that we cover all bases, which we will do here in this book.

What Do Spirit Guides Look Like?

Spirit Guides look just like regular people, like you and me. They come in all shapes and sizes, different heights and different races. Their eye color, age, and hair color varies, and they can be male or female. What does usually differ, however, is the way that they dress, or the way that they present themselves to you visually. You can see your Spirit Guides during dreams, meditation, or past life regression. When you see your Spirit Guide, they tend to dress in the time period of which they are most fond, or in a way that they think might trigger your memory of them.

Although many of you may not remember seeing your Spirit Guide, I am most certain you have probably felt them at one time or another. When you feel them, you

will usually feel them behind you, like someone is standing there and when you turn around there is no one
there. I have never run across anyone that has not had
that feeling at some point in time. Most likely you have
had it when you were alone. Have you ever had that feeling? Most people just brush it off when they realize that
no one is there, or they get freaked out and walk around
backwards for a little while, or sit with their back against
the wall. It is also common for you to feel them behind
you when you are driving in your car, usually over one of
your shoulders. Then you look in the rearview mirror to
make sure that no one is back there.

Why are you more likely to feel your Spirit Guide when
you are alone? Because when you are alone you become
very tuned in, and sensitive, to all of the energy around
you. There is usually nothing else going on to divert your
attention. When people are around you, it is much more
distracting. They are making noise, and you concentrate
on them and what they are doing, or you are engaging in
conversation. If that isn't enough, to make things more
awkward, your Spirit Guides can really be felt at night. If
you are like my friend Dawn, you are probably thinking,
"That's just great! I can never be alone now, especially at
night! Or I am going to have to walk around with a bat
in my hand, and sleep with one eye open!" Just remember Spirit Guides come with love and they are here for
protection and guidance. The reason you can feel them
more at night is because of the thickness of the veil. The

veil is what separates the spirit realm from the physical realm and it is thinner at night; therefore, you are more sensitive to feeling spirit energy at night.

Children are usually very in tune with their Spirit Guides and they feel their presence often. They do not think much of it until they get older, then as young adults, because of their newly formed belief system, it begins to freak them out. So it is then that they will begin to tune it out as much as possible. It is a process most of us go through, unfortunately.

Often when my son was very young, he would see his Spirit Guide around wherever he was at the time. He would mention seeing Frank every now and again when he was around the house. Most nights he would tune in, or become very aware of the presence of his guide. Much of the time his Spirit Guide would be walking on the front porch of our home, or he would show up at the end of his bed, while he was sleeping. He would notice him if he woke up in the middle of the night. Now in most instances, this would startle the majority of kids. They would run tell their parents, everyone would think the house was haunted and they would all want to move! Luckily for him, I was well aware of what he was seeing, and spirits were nothing to be afraid of in our household. They were a part of our life, so it was "normal" to feel them or see them. Needless to say, those experiences were not nearly as scary as they could have been, had the environment been a different one. What I mean by that is, if we had taken on the perspective or belief of spirits being scary.

My son could see his Spirit Guide clearly and he would describe him in great detail. His guide was about six feet tall with dark hair and dark eyes (probably brown, not black or anything). He dressed in a black suit, with a white undershirt, an overcoat, and a fedora hat. The era of dress was consistent with his Spirit Guide's last lifetime here on earth. We know this because when my son was older, I did a past life regression on him (my kids used to love to do this for fun), and he had a very clear memory of being with his Spirit Guide during one of his last lifetimes, sometime in the very early 1900s. He could see that they worked together in that lifetime and he knew roughly where they lived. He knew that his friend saved his life and that they were very good friends throughout that existence.

Dressing in the era of their last existence together may have been an attempt to try and present himself in a manner that my son would recognize him, or potentially trigger some internal memory, as not to frighten him. Or maybe he just liked the suit.

One day I asked my son if he knew why his Spirit Guide was always walking on the front porch, and he said, "Yes, for protection and to watch over me!" A few nights after that conversation, his Spirit Guide began talking to me. At first it sounded a little far away, but then the voice became louder. It sounded like I was listening to an old radio that was mostly tuned in, but still a little fuzzy or static. He told me he was my son's Spirit Guide. I knew that he came to me because I had asked my son questions about him. That's what spirits do, they come in when you think about them; you may not be aware of this, but it is true. So, I asked him what his name was. In a chipper voice he responded, "Frank." Then he waited. I was surprised at the personality that came through in his voice, it was strong yet happy. I guess I expected his voice to be more serious or down to business sounding, but it wasn't. So I asked him why he was here.

He answered with a slight chuckle, "I am here for protection." Kind of like, you already know this, but I will be happy to confirm it for you! It was interesting that he told me exactly what my son already knew; kids are very good at receiving communication from their Spirit Guides. We had a few more words, and then Frank faded out. Which brings us to the next chapter...

How Do Spirit Guides Communicate?

So this brings us to the next chapter and something I find very interesting but people don't ask about very often: how do Spirit Guides communicate? I think this question is not asked very much because most people assume that they know the answer already. The interesting thing is, most of the time their assumptions are wrong. When I teach this subject in a class or a lecture, the students often realize that they are actually quite confused on how this spirit communication thing happens. People are often under the impression that Spirit Guides communicate with you through just one avenue, and when and if it happens you'll know it. I think the only reason for this assumption is that most of the time you just haven't given it too much thought. Because for some of you, the idea of thinking that you actually have some sort of control over how you communicate with your Spirit Guide probably seems a little far-fetched. Truthfully, some of you might even be on the fence about whether or not to believe in this whole Spirit Guide thing in the first place. But think about it, you really need to know more about how the communication process works in order to rule out any of those things anyway!

Spirit Guides communicate with you in various ways. Some are more common than others, and some of these avenues can have a very subtle approach to them, especially at first. In other words, it is important for you to be aware of the communication process in order to receive the information. Otherwise, you may just think that you are having random thoughts and disregard them when you are actually receiving information from your Spirit Guide.

Here are the most common ways Spirit Guides communicate with you, in no particular order:

#1 Through Telepathy

The first avenue I would like to address, and one of the most common ways for a Spirit Guide to communicate with you, is through telepathy. Telepathy is when you receive information by hearing or seeing something in your mind, or what is called "your mind's eye" that another person (or in this case a spirit) has intentionally put there as an attempt to communicate with you. In other words, they are trying to relay a message to you. It can be in the form of words, letters, pictures, or a combination of all of these things. Telepathy is something Spirit Guides will utilize in order to communicate short bursts of information to you. For instance, if your Spirit Guide thinks it would be useful for you to buy a certain book. Maybe that book contains information that would be useful to you. Out of nowhere that book might pop into your head, an image of the book, or the title to the book. Or maybe you are trying to think of a great place to take a vacation, and out of nowhere a destination you never even thought of pops into your head. These are just examples; just remember it is used for short bursts of information, as well as yes or no kind of information.

#2 Blocks of Thought

Another popular way of receiving spirit communication is by receiving blocks of thought. This happens when the information being relayed to you is too much information to give you in just a few pictures or words. Imagine it like this: when you download information from the Internet onto your computer, you get a bunch of information compiled together giving you an overall picture real quick. This avenue is usually utilized with people who are more advanced and know where it is coming from. Also, anyone who is really tapped into his or her creative side will utilize this avenue often. Artists, musicians, and writers use this process a lot. They will receive whole concepts this way, then they can fill in all of the little details themselves. Things like an idea for a song, or a vision of a character, or a plot for a book or movie. They will receive the overall vision and then they can elaborate upon it. As a psychic, this is an avenue that my Spirit Guides often utilize. When I meet someone, I get huge blocks of information on that particular person. Things like what type of person they are, things they are struggling with now or in the past, what their intentions are, etcetera.

#3 A "Knowing"

This is a bit different, and in my experience, not everyone utilizes this gift. It is tied into a psychic ability people can have called claircognizance. Claircognizance is sometimes used in conjunction with other avenues of communication as a way of "confirming" the information you are receiving in from your Spirit Guide. This "knowing" is a feeling you will get across your entire being, on a soul level. It is when you already know something is true as if it has already happened. You feel it in the body and it is something you know as fact. You will know immediately if you utilize this form of communication, because it is hard to explain to people who have not experienced it. If this does not sound familiar to you, this is most likely an avenue which you will not use.

#4 Dreams and Meditation

Communication through dreams and meditation is also quite common, when you remember them. Many times people have a hard time remembering what information they receive during the night. When you fall asleep you naturally align yourself spiritually; in fact, this is why you need to sleep. It's not just to rest your body. It has been scientifically proven that your body gets enough rest during times of sitting throughout the day that it does not require a long period of sleep to recover. Sleep, however, has been programmed into your Soul DNA to make sure that you have a consistent time each day in which you allow yourself to spiritually align again. Why? Because even if you were very aware of the requirements of your spiritual being needing to be in spiritual alignment at least once everyday, what are the chances that everyone would do it and do it consistently? About zero! That being said, you do it anyway and it's called sleep. During this time, your belief system comes down, and you naturally reach higher consciousness. When you reach higher consciousness, you are able to shift dimensions with ease and maneuver the spirit world effortlessly. You can see loved ones who have passed over. This is why many times when you awaken from a dream where you have seen or visited with a loved one who has passed, you can't explain why but it feels very different, very real. Then you wake up, your belief system is promptly restored to the physical realm, and you call it a dream.

My daughter used to see loved ones all of the time during the night and they would have long conversations with her. She would wake up and tell me about her "visits." See, in our household they are visits, because we are all very well aware of the dimensional shifting that takes place, but to other people they are mistaken for dreams. So during this dream state you can get quite a lot of information from your spirit guide. As far as meditation is concerned, when done properly, your belief system is also left behind and you begin to touch lightly upon dimensional shifting. When this takes place, the spirit communication will become part of the process if you wish.

#5 Hearing With the "Inner Ear"

You may or may not have heard this term before: "inner ear." This is a term you will become very familiar with if you are learning to develop your intuition or spirit communication. What this means is that you hear things in your head from the "inner ear" so it sounds like it is coming from within your inner being, instead of outside of your being like when you hear with the outer ear. For instance, you know how you can recall a conversation that you had or a song that you heard recently and you can hear it just by remembering it? That is what it is like to hear something with your "inner ear," only it is not something that you are reaching for or you are trying to remember. When in a very relaxed state it is information that is received, or heard, within. You may ask, "Well how do I know that it is not just my own thinking?" Because, it is not information that is reached for, it is just allowed or received. This process of hearing with the inner ear usually takes quite a bit of training and confirmation. It requires time and training because in order for this type of communication to be effective, you need to develop a certain level of trust that you are receiving information from a source outside of yourself, and not just making things up. Building that kind of trust takes some time and it can be developed with training.

This "inner ear" type of communication is very common with psychics and mediums; often they hear spirits with their inner ear. They begin to develop this skill when they realize other people are not hearing what they are hearing. Like I mentioned before, it takes some training to develop the trust needed to affectively work with the inner ear.

#6 Audibly With the "Outer Ear"

Lastly, we have audible communication with your Spirit Guides. This is just like it sounds only worse! When you hear your Spirit Guide audibly, you can hear them just like you hear someone talking to you, only their voice is usually louder, crisper and more startling. See, when tone or sound travels between dimensions, it comes through with a very unique sound. It is very crisp to your eardrum and you immediately identify it as something you have not heard before. This is your Spirit Guide's least favorite way to communicate with you for all of these reasons.

To give you an idea of what it is like, I will tell you about the first audible experience that I had with my Spirit Guide. Many years ago, when I was very young, I was in a large department store shopping by myself. During this time of my life, my family and I were in the midst of dealing with a very unstable family member. Needless to say, it was very difficult, and it was definitely taking a toll on everyone. While shopping, out of nowhere, I heard the most authoritative voice say, "Get out now!" The voice was so loud and crisp that I was frozen in my tracks. I couldn't breathe, my heart began to race like someone was chasing me, and my legs felt like concrete so I couldn't move. I looked behind me because it sounded as if the voice had come from someone standing directly behind me. I was scared to turn around, but as I did, I realized no one was there. So I looked around, and at the door, but to my surprise, everyone seemed fine. There was no urgency at all! I immediately got my bearings after what felt like ten very long minutes (but in actuality was probably about twenty seconds), and realized from the tone of the voice that it was not a person, but my Spirit Guide. Still terrified, I was looking around to see what could be so dangerous that I had to get out! Was there going to be a robbery? What was happening? When my eyes scanned the front door for the second time, I saw the troubled family member entering the store. This may not seem like a big deal to others, but at the time, the stress I was under was affecting my health, so I was very grateful to have avoided this encounter.

Now to be fair, I have also heard Frank audibly, like I would hear a regular person talking to me. However, because I have had previous experience with this type of communication, I knew immediately from the tone that it was a Spirit Guide. During the encounter in the department store, my guide was trying to contact me in an urgent way, so I would be more apt to listen, and not just blow it off, or not take the message seriously. With Frank the matter was not so urgent, so his voice was not as powerful. Because there was no sense of urgency in his voice, the tone was also not so loud. After the department store experience, however, I did ask my Spirit Guides not to scare the daylights out of me like that again. So now when they wish to talk with me audibly, they whisper or speak lightly as not to shock my system. I much prefer it that way.

Hearing your Spirit Guide audibly is not very common, even for psychics and mediums. In fact, I do not know many people at all who have heard their Spirit Guides this way. Most psychics and mediums receive information in some of the other forms that we have talked about, such as words, pictures, blocks of thought, or inner ear. So do not get discouraged if you have not heard or do not hear your Spirit Guides audibly; it is rare. In my opinion you might even want to be happy about not hearing them that way!

What Is It Like To Receive Communications From Your Spirit Guide?

I feel this is a very important step and it is often left out when you are learning about the spirit communication process. It is helpful when you know what it "feels" like to communicate with your Spirit Guide in order to help you develop your communication skills. When you become familiar with this process, then you better know what to expect when receiving information from them.

This is a really great time to give you some exercises to try.

Exercise #1
Observe the Alpha State

As you fall asleep at night, notice your relaxed mental state. When you find your mind wandering wildly and you begin to see dreamlike images in your mind's eye, you are in what is referred to as the Alpha state. Pay attention to what this Alpha state feels like whenever you go to sleep, and learn to recognize this state when you are meditating or during times of relaxation. Really observe the dreamlike images by allowing them in, do not force anything, observe the state of allowing, the state of no resistance. This is the key, relax and allow, relax and allow.

These Alpha experiences are very similar to what many mediums experience when communicating with spirits. When you do this exercise you will become familiar with the state that you will experience when communicating with spirits. During this time, you naturally let your guard down as you are preparing yourself to be spiritually aligned, through sleep. As part of the process you allow pictures to come in, with no resistance. This is an ability everyone has; it is just that not many people realize how useful it is. By doing this exercise you will become consciously aware of what it is like to receive and recognize the faint mental impressions that occur during spirit communication. You will become very aware of the state of allowing, with no attachments to what is coming in and what is going out. You should do this every night until you begin to feel the resistance to spirit communication diminish during your waking hours.

Exercise #2
Visualizing In the "Mind's Eye"

As we talked about before, your Spirit Guide's first and favorite choice of communication is through visions and words, via telepathy. So I would like you to read this and then do the exercise.

You see through your mind's eye all of the time, you probably just called it remembering. Remembering uses the same process of seeing in your "mind's eye." What you are "seeing" is what separates a memory from spirit communication. When you remember something you are seeing something in your mind's eye that you were a part of, hence, have a memory of; in other words, you were there so you remember it. When a Spirit Guide is trying to communicate with you through telepathy or your "mind's eye," you see it as if you remember it, only you never had that particular experience to remember. So it is new information that you see through the "mind's eye."

To practice this process, I want you to visualize something in your mind's eye. It could be a person or an object like a four leaf clover. Think of something and then close your eyes and concentrate for a few seconds on this image. See it and observe it, the color, the shape, and the size.

Then I want you to imagine seeing a red rose. I want you to look at it and observe it, the vivid color, the shape, and the size. See the thorns and observe how they would hurt if you touch them. Then I want you to touch the pedals of the rose, feel the softness, and observe how they feel like velvet. The next thing that I want you to do is to smell the rose, smell how strong the aroma is. I would like you to spend a few minutes observing the flower with all of your senses.

Then lastly, picture in your mind somewhere that you have always wanted to visit. Anywhere in the world, even if you are scared to go there, just imagine that you are there right now. Look around, what do you see? Are there people? Are you outside or inside? What do you hear? What do you smell? Spend some time at this place, seeing, hearing, smelling, and observing with all of your senses.

The purpose of this exercise is it helps you to become familiar with how it "feels" to see things in the mind's eye. These exercises are also designed to be a part of the training process for your "etheric" body, or spiritual body. The same way you exercise and train your physical body for something physical, you must also exercise and train your spiritual body in order to help you perform spiritual tasks as well.

Exercise #3
Hearing With Your "Inner Ear"

This exercise is going to be similar to the prior exercise. I also want you to read through this exercise before you try it.

Hearing with the inner ear is going to be very similar to seeing with the mind's eye. You have done this many times before through your memory, only instead of seeing something, it involves hearing something. Since I have explained the similarities once before, I am going to get right into the exercise. I want you to remember the last conversation that you had; what did the other person say? What did you say? Hear the tone of the conversation, hear the emotion, and observe what was said.

The next thing I would like you to do is to try and remember a song you have recently heard on the radio. Listen to it, hear the beat, hear the words, and enjoy the music. Let this song play for a while. Practice this exercise with different things, you can even do it with rain or wind or the sound of the ocean. Observe this state and what it feels like to hear with the inner ear. Become familiar with it.

Now that you have observed the Alpha state, seeing with your mind's eye and hearing with the inner ear, you can have a better understanding of the way in which Spirit Guides will often show you something, and you will have a better understanding of how spirit communication works. Now that you have a better understanding of this process and how it works, you can hone these skills so that they become quite affective.

Just remember that when you are first learning the communication process, however, the communication will most likely seem very light and subtle or even faint. When this happens it may feel a little difficult at first and this leaves some people feeling frustrated. But please note that this is a process. You have spent many, many years trying to block out any spirit communication. So you have to learn to tear down the very wall you have spent much time and many years building. However, as your sensitivity begins to develop again, as it will if you are consistent, these messages will seem anything but subtle. It takes time, so be patient. I worked on developing strong spirit communication skills for close to five years when I was young and I am a psychic! But I was very focused on becoming the best spirit communicator that I could be!

Chakras and Spirit Communication

Here is an area where I feel most people fail when teaching about spirit communication. They either forget about it, assume you know it (big mistake), or they truly don't understand the correlation themselves between the chakra system and spirit communication as teachers. Your chakra system is a very important part of the spirit communication system. It is vital for you to pay attention to and understand your chakra system when you are developing spirit communication. If you know about chakras already, DO NOT skip over this section, as 99 percent of people do not actually know where their chakra systems lie, and this is important for you to know.

However, I am going to quickly run over the basics first. What is your chakra system? It is energy centers where your physical body and your etheric body meet. Your etheric body is your "spiritual body." You have seven main chakras on the body and they each do different things. See diagram below:

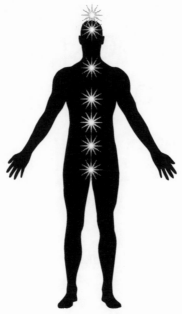

Now, even I did not realize myself until I started teaching spirit communication classes that most people do not know where their chakras centers are on their own body. As you can see from the diagram, the chakra system is right down the center of the body, which is correct; however, the chakra centers themselves do not lie in the center of your body (front to back) but they are actually near your back or near your spine. Most people see the diagrams and/or have read things that say they are down the center of the body, and assume this also means of equal distance from the front of your body as well as from the back of your body. Many people believe the chakra system starts at the center of the top of your head and extends down through the center of the body, and this is not where the meeting point is (where your physical and etheric body meet). The chakras do extend out to the center of your body and even beyond, but the meeting point is located near your spinal column. Why is this important? Because you will utilize the chakra system during spirit communication; in fact, it is an important component in the process. Primarily you will be working with chakras four, five, and six, and this meeting point is something with which you will become very familiar during this process. It is also very important to developing your sensitivity level and learning control as you advance.

Since this is not a book about the chakra system I am only going to briefly touch upon them, in order to give you the information that you need. Chakra is "Sanskrit" for wheel or disk. They are spinning wheels of energy, or "vortexes." They filter energy from the environment and allow only matching vibrations in and rid the rest. It is where psychic energy travels from the spirit realm to you in the physical realm. There are seven main chakra centers and they are each responsible for different things in your spiritual and physical bodies. Each of them is also represented by a color.

1st Chakra
Root Chakra (Color: Red)

- Earth chakra, it is your foundation
- Glands: adrenals
- Other Body Parts: legs, feet, bones, large intestine, teeth
- Malfunction: weight problems, hemorrhoids, constipation, sciatica, degenerative arthritis, knee troubles
- Purpose: to ground you like a lightning rod (very important in spiritual work), plugs your energy into the earth's energy. Grounding is a coping mechanism for stress.
- Survival chakra

2nd Chakra
Desire Chakra (Color: Orange)

- Water chakra
- Glands: ovaries, testicles
- Body Parts: womb, genitals, kidney, bladder, circulatory system
- Malfunction: impotence, frigidity, uterine, bladder or kidney trouble, stiff lower back
- Purpose: to let go and flow (movement). The center of sexuality, emotions, desire, sensation, pleasure, movement and nurturance. Related to the moon and its pull on energy.

- Clairsentience/empath is the psychic sense of the second chakra

3rd Chakra
Power Chakra (Color: Yellow)

- Fire chakra
- Glands: pancreas, adrenals
- Body Parts: digestive system, muscles
- Malfunction: ulcers, diabetes, hypoglycemia, digestive disorders
- Purpose: transformation and personal power
- Intuition sits in this chakra—gut feeling

4th Chakra
The Center of Love (Color: Green)

- Air chakra
- Glands: thymus
- Body Parts: lungs, heart, pericardium, arms, hands
- Malfunctions: asthma, high blood pressure, heart disease, lung disease
- Purpose: compassion and love
- Higher consciousness elevates and expands the heart chakra; therefore, it is sometimes utilized during spirit communication. Empaths also utilize this chakra.

5th Chakra
Communication/Creativity Chakra (Color: Blue)

- Sound chakra
- Glands: thyroid, parathyroid
- Body Parts: neck, shoulders, arms, hands
- Malfunction: sore throat, stiff neck, colds, thyroid problems, hearing problems
- Purpose: communication and creativity, communication through sound, vibration, self-expression, and creativity. It includes listening, speaking, writing, telepathy and any of the arts. As your creative chakra, artists and musicians utilize this chakra consistently.
- Channeling information from the spirit realm, channels utilize this chakra almost always during spirit communication.

6th Chakra
Seeing and Intuition (Color: Indigo)

- Intuition and psychic ability chakra
- Glands: pineal
- Body Parts: eyes
- Malfunction: blindness, headaches, nightmares, eyestrain, blurred vision
- Purpose: development of psychic abilities
- Clairvoyance or clear seeing

7th Chakra
Consciousness or Understanding Chakra
(Color: Violet to White)

- Thought chakra
- Gland: pituitary
- Body Parts: cerebral cortex, central nervous system
- Malfunctions: depression, alienation, confusion, boredom, apathy, inability to learn
- Purpose: this chakra is the seat of enlightenment
- The function is thought and knowing or claircognizance

So now that you know the basics, you need to pay particular attention to chakras four, five, and six. Those are the ones in between the shoulder blades, the upper back and back of your neck, and back of your head. Why? Because when you are working with spirit communication those chakras open and they open wide!

When I first really started to develop my spirit communication to an advanced level, something really threw me off. I would be walking around constantly feeling like there was a huge gapping hole in the back of my neck and sometimes I could feel a hole between my shoulder blades as well. I could tell that they were clearly two different holes; they did not run into each other and they felt very separate to me. They felt so big it seemed as if someone could put a fist in there. The weird thing was that I knew there was no hole, so what was going on? Well, most teachers do not teach about this particular experience because they do not know themselves, or they assume and take for granted that you know what this big gapping hole is. But in either case this is the "meeting point" which I mentioned earlier; this is the place where your two bodies meet. The feeling is your chakra centers opening wide and activating to allow information to be received from the spiritual realm and your spiritual body and transferring this information to your physical body. When you become more advanced you can learn to open and close those centers at will, but when you are first developing you may walk around feeling "open" in the back. They will activate at random and it can be really annoying when you are at the movie theater! You can feel this "opening" behind your head, neck, or between your shoulder blades. You could feel them open all at once, or it could be one at a time, it makes no difference. The way that they open and which ones open at what time is unique to each individual.

Something else you might experience, besides the energetic gapping holes in your back (as if that is not enough), is when your fifth or sixth chakra begins to activate, you may also start to heat up. Channels experience this sensation often when they communicate with spirits. What do I mean by heat up? Well, usually around your ears you will become very hot and tingly. You will feel heat stemming from the inside of your being, and your skin will become red to reflect the heat. You will also feel hot to the touch. I am a natural channel, not just a psychic, so this is something that I experience. This was also new to me when it first began to happen. When I am working with spirits, I begin to feel the heat first and then the hole, but the heat seems to precede the feeling of the hole. The heat starts around the back of my neck or ears and as I continue to raise my vibration, I begin to turn red from the heat. My ears heat up so hot that people say it feels like I am burning up. When I am really heating up it will run from my ears all the way down my neck. At first, when I was young, it weirded me out! I couldn't figure out why I was getting so hot, especially because developing your skills happens at random, not just during spirit communication. Now that I am more skilled in the process, I have total control; I can raise my vibration and open those centers at will and close them down at will. Now I enjoy it; I become very relaxed when I start to heat up. I am in what people in sports call a "zone." Heat is a very good indicator of a channeling ability. I have heated up so much from writing this book right now you could probably fry an egg on my neck…but I am not going to confirm it!

10 Tips For Working With Spirit Guides and Spirits

This section is going to contain a list of ten simple tips to help you when you are learning to develop your Spirit Guide communication. These are important and though they are in no particular order, they are equally important!

Tip #1
Know Who You Are Working With

When you begin to work on developing your Spirit Guide communication, you are opening the door to the spirit world so you will naturally open the door to other spirits as well. This is something that is important for you to have knowledge about and something you should be aware of. If you are not aware of this, you could receive information from spirits who are *not* your Spirit Guide. Even spirits who do not have your best interest at heart; yes, as much as I never wanted to believe in bad intentioned spirits, it is true, it can happen! This is why you should never, ever, play with a Ouija board. To avoid working with spirits who are not your Spirit Guide, there are a few things you should know to help you tell the difference, as well as steps you should take to specifically ask for the spirit contact to be with your Spirit Guide or spirits of the highest vibration. That being said, I will give you some simple steps to help you avoid attracting undesirables.

Tip #2
Say a Prayer First

When you are trying to contact or connect with your Spirit Guide, always, always say a prayer first and ask for only the highest vibration of spirits who are working for your greatest good to come through. Something along the lines of, "I would like to make contact with my Spirit Guide, I am asking for my Spirit Guide to come in and make contact with me. Only the highest vibration of spirits are allowed to make contact with me, those who come from the white light of the Holy Spirit, amen," or, "I would only like to speak with my Spirit Guide, who comes with the highest vibration and from the white light of the Holy Spirit, all other spirits are not allowed to make contact with me." You get the idea.

Tip #3
Spirits Are Attracted To Us When We Think Of Them

Yes, it is true, when you think of a spirit they tend to come in. So if you feel a spirit around you during a meditation, you can ask them to show themselves to you or ask them if they have any messages for you and just feel their presence. When you ask them a question, make sure to stay in the state of allowing, in order for the pictures to come in. If there are no pictures, then just feel their presence and enjoy the feeling of them making themselves known to you on the physical plane. Feeling their presence does just as much as allowing as far as strengthening the connection. For example, if you see a spirit in your mind's eye, use all of your senses. Feel them, allow the vision of them to form, and listen to hear if they are saying anything. Spirits are attracted to you when you think of them because when you think of them, it is like you are calling for them. They hear the call in the spiritual realm and they come to you. This is also why it is very common for you to feel loved ones who have passed over when you are thinking of them. If you are thinking of someone and feel their presence, close your eyes and just concentrate on that feeling, just feel them. Then allow any pictures to float in and out with no judgment, because they may try to tell you something. Many times it is just that they love you or they are watching over you, something along those lines. They do not give you lotto numbers!

Tip #4
Spirit Guides Do Not Come To You or Present Themselves To You With Physical Disabilities

Generally spirits in the spirit world do not have any physical disabilities they may have had here on earth. If you see a spirit who is deformed or you perceive them as angry, confused, or unhappy, you may be encountering an earth bound spirit or what people like to call a ghost. When you are learning to develop your spirit communication skills, it is wise to avoid contact with such spirits. If you encounter a spirit who makes you uncomfortable, you should repeat the prayer for protection, a prayer like I mentioned in tip #2, until you feel them leave or you feel comfortable. Also, imagine a barrier of white light surrounding you that only the highest vibration spirits can penetrate. Lastly ask for your Angels to come in, and remove any low vibration spirits from your area and take them away. After your Angels come in, the uncomfortable spirit should be gone. When you become more experienced and advanced in communicating with spirits, you may want to try to help earth bound spirits by encouraging them to go to the white light so that they can transition to the "Other Side." You can ask for Angles or loved ones to come in to try and help them make the transition. There is also a process of explaining to them that they are no longer physically alive, but for now, it is good just to concentrate on working with your Spirit Guide.

Tip #5
Write Things/Experiences Down

It is a good practice for you to write down all of your experiences afterwards. Often, you may find that a message will become clearer when you write it down. During the moment you are receiving information you are in the process of allowing, or in a state of no resistance. When you are doing this, you are working more with the right brain. When you write things down, you will switch into a different mode of remembering and analyzing; this is where you will switch from right brain to left brain. When you make this transition from right brain to left brain, sometimes it can help you to remember things or little details you may have missed otherwise. Write your experiences down as if you are writing a letter to someone else. Explain your experience in great detail so when you read it later, you can recall the experience more vividly. During this writing process you may actually receive even more information and sometimes it can turn into an automatic writing session without you even being aware of it. This process allows you to move from right brain to left brain more fluidly because you are still tuned into the spirit realm and you are not so focused on your belief system. So when you begin to write, your barriers are already down. All kinds of amazing information can come through this way (I have an exercise for this coming up).

Tip #6
Never Do Anything You Would Not Normally Do

What I mean by this is exactly what it says; never do anything that you would not otherwise do because you think a spirit told you to do it, or that you are being "guided" in some way. Spirits do not usually "tell" you to do something in particular. They will not tell you that you should get a divorce or make an investment of some kind. When you are communicating with your Spirit Guide it is more like they are showing you what path is best to take and why. You are meant to receive this information, weigh it with all the other knowledge you have, and then make a decision. Your Spirit Guide's role is to help you consider all things physical and spiritual before guiding you towards a decision. They are here to offer you spiritual guidance; their job is not to be a dictator. View it as more of a joint collaboration than being told what to do. Low vibration spirits, on the other hand, can and in some instances will try to influence you into making a certain decision; decisions which are meant to cause you issues or problems. Low vibration spirits can have bad intentions. In the beginning you may have difficulty distinguishing your Spirit Guide from other spirits. So if the information feels good and right in your heart, then it is pretty safe to say it is good information. If it just doesn't feel right, then don't jump into anything without further consideration.

Tip #7
Physical Sensations Are Common

You may feel physical sensations around your head, neck, ears, back, or in other parts of your body. This can be an indication of your Spirit Guides working with healing energy to give you a healing or working on your electromagnetic system in order to help you become more sensitive to receive spirit communications. The interesting thing is that these sensations usually come after or between working on your spirit communication and development, instead of during (besides the heating up that I talked about in the chakra chapter). Some of these sensations can include things like:

- Tingling Sensation
- Prickly Sensation
- Feeling Hot/Cold
- Hot Spots

Assuming that you have a clean bill of health, if you are working on developing your spirit communication skills, these things can be common. What confuses people is that these sensations can occur at any time, and it's not usually during spirit contact. A couple of these things used to happen to me when I was younger and working hard on my own communication skills. I used to get a prickly hot and cold feeling all over my body, for a while I thought it was a sign of dehydration. But, I drank lots of water and had regular checkups, and physically I was fine. These prickly sensations would usually last about one to two hours and go away. At the time, I would also usually have a "knowing" or visions of being worked on energetically by my Spirit Guides. It seemed as if my electrical system, or electromagnetic system, was being rewired, and in an odd way, that's what it felt like. This would usually last a couple of days then disappear for several months. I do not get them anymore. Another thing that would happen is, I would get hot spots all over my body, accompanied with the same visions. It felt like someone was holding a lighter to my skin, only from the inside. I would have many of these hot spots going on at one time all over my body. They didn't hurt, but it was really annoying! Why does this happen? It's like I mentioned before, when you are truly committed to working with your Spirit Guides, your physical system usually needs some adjustment. So your Spirit Guides work with your inner "electrical" system in order to make it possible for you to raise your vibration to a very high level. Imagine that you have an old electrical system in your house and you rewire it so you can install a whole new communication system; it's like that. If this does happen to you, you will know, because it feels like it sounds, like you are being rewired! Don't worry about it though, it doesn't hurt, it's just a strange feeling.

Tip #8
Be Consistent

If you really want to develop your ability to work with your Spirit Guides, consistency is the key! Can you develop this ability without consistency? Yes; however, it takes longer and you will not become as advanced. When I say consistent, I do not mean it has to disrupt your daily routine, simply make it a part of your daily routine. In other words, make it part of your morning ritual or nighttime ritual or both. I used to do my Spirit Guide communication meditation every morning for about two years straight. I would get up an extra twenty to thirty minutes early, take a shower, eat, get ready, then use the extra time I had to do the meditation. I began to enjoy it very much. Starting my day this way made a difference on how I felt; I felt calmer, and I began to see a correlation between meditation in the morning and my day going smoother. On the days I didn't do the meditation, things seemed to be a little more jumbled, and things didn't seem to go as smooth, so I got to the point where I really looked forward to it. I tried to do it every day, but obviously that is hard to do, so I was happy if I could do it five times a week. What consistency does is it sets a time when your Spirit Guide knows you are looking for them. Plus, it regulates your brainwave pattern making it easier to go into the Alpha state quicker. You do not have to do the Spirit Guide meditation every day; alternately, you could do the writing exercise (which I include in the exercise portion).

Tip #9
Meditation

If you choose to go the writing route to further develop your spirit communication skills, tip #9 is very, very important. Just to be clear, I want to tell you exactly what meditation is and why you need to do it (like I said before, I want to cover all bases). Meditation is a practice of sitting quietly, while regulating your breath using intone mantras or visualization in attempts to harmonize your mind, body, and soul. Why is this important? Well, because meditation is really effective in clearing out mind clutter as well as energetic clutter. It is knocking out two birds with one stone, so to speak, on a spiritual and physical level.

You clean your house, take showers, eat right, and maintain your physical health by getting the proper rest, etcetera. Well, it is equally important to your physical and spiritual health to keep your mind and your energetic field as clutter free as possible. This will allow you to operate at your most efficient level.

There have been some extensive studies done on meditation and the most noteworthy finding of these studies seemed to show in the EEG measuring of brain wave patterns. During your waking consciousness, brain waves are random and chaotic. The brain usually operates with different wavelengths from the front to the back of the brain, and from hemisphere to hemisphere. Meditation changes this drastically. Subjects in meditation show increased Alpha waves and these waves continue to increase throughout the duration of the meditation. Also, the front and the back of the brain begin to synchronize as well as the left and the right hemispheres. In other words, the different areas of your brain begin to work together synchronistically! There has been documented research, which shows that the daily practice of meditation creates a more efficient, integrated brain functioning. After a few months, this integration in the brain is not just noticed during the meditation state but during daily activity as well. I can personally attest to this, as it helped me learn how to go into the Alpha state quickly, and at will, for when I do psychic readings.

Health wise, meditation has also been linked to lowering blood pressure, helping with anxiety and depression just to name a few. Not to mention the spiritual aspects of raising your vibration, intuitive development and raising your consciousness.

Here is a meditation exercise I designed to help you work more efficiently with the Universal Laws. I suggest doing some type of meditation at least once a day, I personally recommend for you to do it in the morning if you only have time for one meditation. Morning meditation, I have noticed, definitely sets the tone of your day.

Meditation Exercise

Before you begin, find a quiet place where you will not be disturbed. You will be using a chair for this meditation, so find a comfortable chair to sit in, then place both feet flat on the floor.

1)   Define what it is that you want to achieve in your meditation. This is a very important step whether it is calmness, joy, better health, or happiness; whatever it is that you desire. This is very important because intent is what actually creates things whether it is in the Spiritual or Physical realm.

2)   Sit comfortably in a chair or in an upright position in a quiet place.

3)   Close your eyes and concentrate on your breathing. Slow your breathing to a relaxed state.

4)   When your breathing is rhythmic, concentrate on relaxing all of the muscles in your body.

5)   Imagine that your spine is like a string on a musical instrument. Imagine that this string or cord attaches all of your chakras together, from your root chakra to your crown chakra.

6)   Visualize this string or cord vibrating. Imagine that you are in control of how fast or slow the vibration is. Next raise this vibration to the highest level of vibration that you can achieve.

7)   When you are vibrating at a high level, imagine that you can see a river above your body. Imagine that this river is the river of the Universe. This river of the Universe contains all the Universal energy.

8)   Then visualize that you are attaching your energy to the Universal River. When you attach your energy with the Universal River, feel yourself flowing in harmony with the Universal Laws.

9)   From that state imagine whatever it is that you desire being attracted to you. Imagine that your desires are coming to you as if you are a human magnet.

10) Remain in this state until you feel a sense of completion, and then release this image into the Universe.

You should not set a time limit on how long or short your meditation should be, just do what feels right. For many people it will change each day, some days it might be twenty minutes while others it might be two minutes. The consistency of meditation (how many times a week, etcetera) is more important than how long the meditation is. In my opinion, meditation time should be adjusted to fit your own personal needs depending on what is happening in your life at the time.

Tip #10
Be Patient!

This is the one tip I think people struggle with the most: being patient. Like I said before, I spent two years consistently working on my spirit communication development and doing the Spirit Guide communication meditation at least four to five times a week. I spent three more years advancing and developing that skill to the best of my ability, a total of five years! Not to mention spirit communication is what I do for a living, so I practice my skill for many, many hours every single day. Does that mean you have to do what I did or do now? Absolutely not! Unless, of course, you want to tell other people what their Spirit Guides wish them to know, or what Grandma has to say, for a living. But do not try this a few times and think, "This doesn't work!" You need to be committed and realistic, and know it's a process. It's not easy what I do; if everyone did it, there would be no need for psychics or mediums. In other words, it's like anything else: if you want to learn to play golf, you take lessons and you practice. If you want to learn to surf, you take lessons and you practice. If you want to learn to ski, you take lessons and you practice. You get the point!

Communicating With Spirit Guides Through Writing

Utilizing writing techniques as a means of developing your spirit communication is a way of channeling your Spirit Guides or higher self that is not so scary, as well as utilizing your left and right brains which can be more comfortable for some people. It is a process of allowing them to speak through you in blocks of thought, the mind's eye, inner ear, or whatever works, through writing it down instead of speaking it. This practice is very effective because people get caught up in getting their "ideas" or channeled information down on paper or on the computer instead of analyzing where it is coming from. There are a few different ways you can do this. One way is through automatic writing. Many great books have been written this way; in fact, I wrote large portions of my book *Soul DNA* this way. I would sit at the computer and go okay, what information do you have for me today? Then after a few minutes it would just start coming in. It would come in so fast that I did not even have a chance to read it. I would just write and write for hours. Then I would read it later and think, "Wow, this is great stuff!" Many people write songs this way, or poems; it's a wonderful tool and effective when utilized. This first exercise is to learn how to develop your automatic writing skill.

Exercise #1
Automatic Writing

1) Sit down with the intention of writing about anything you are spiritually interested in, or about something that is important in your life, such as problems you might be having that you would like to address.

2) As always, you should start any Spirit Guide communication process with a prayer asking for only the highest vibration spirits to be allowed to make contact with you, only spirits who come from the white light of the Holy Spirit. Then you want to imagine a white light coming down from above and surrounding you and protecting you from any low entity spirits.

3) After you prepare yourself, you can begin writing, on paper or at a keyboard. Start by thinking of a question then remove yourself and allow yourself to answer from an "outsider's perspective." As you begin this outsider view, it allows you to remove your own beliefs and tap into the spirit world by allowing new information to come through you in your writing. This detachment is a learning process; however, once you get in the habit of it and know what it "feels" like, you will be able to do it at will. It takes a little while to develop a skill in automatic writing; it can take months and sometimes years, so do not get impatient. But if you like to write, it is well worth it!

4) When you get into the flow of writing, do not stop and read it or edit it. Continue to write all of the information that comes into your mind until you feel the flow stop, or until you need a break. If you try and stop to read it, this will shift you from right brain to left brain and puts a hiccup in the process. It will then take some time to reestablish the flow. Allow the process to flow naturally until it is done.

5) When you become "tuned in" while writing, normally you will have some physical sensations. They may seem very subtle at first, but they will become stronger as you develop. You will become very relaxed; the feeling is very similar to being in a meditative state. You may also feel hot or begin to turn red as your

chakras start to open. Writing is a form of channeling, so this is very common. Pay close attention to any physical sensations you have when practicing any spirit communication exercises. If you pay attention, sometimes you will feel the physical sensations come first, then you will know that your body is preparing itself for spirit communication.

6) This process is a development process, so remember that you will have to put in some time writing in order to see results. If you enjoy writing, excellent! If you do not enjoy writing and you just want to advance in spirit communication, do not force yourself to do this. There are all kinds of ways to advance, which I am covering in this book. You do not need to do all of the exercises here in this book; in fact, I do not even recommend it. You should just do the ones that suit you best, or that you are most interested in.

Spirit Guide Communication Through Dreaming

Dreaming is actually one of the easiest, most natural ways to connect with the spirit world. For over fifty years scientists have continued to study the science behind dreaming. The only really, really solid reason they have come up with for the reason behind why we dream is because we get sleepy! It has had scientists baffled for years, and will continue to do so, as they are not looking for the answers they are seeking in the right place. They have failed to study dreaming/sleeping from a spiritual aspect, as they are scientists, studying from the physical side. From a physical perspective they have proven that we get enough rest during the day from sitting at our desks, driving our cars, and sitting while watching TV, that sleep is not required for our physical body.

It is, however, required for our spiritual health. We have been programmed through our Soul DNA, or spiritual genetic system, to spiritually align ourselves every single day, and it's called sleep. Sleep is how we spiritually align ourselves. What is spiritual alignment? It is a time in which we break away from the physical realm and its limitations, to explore other dimensions, other realities, and become spiritually free with no limitations. We astral travel, we have complete access to the spirit world, and we reach higher consciousness. It is, and should be, viewed as an extension of your reality. Nowadays, you are told from a very young age that your dreams are like a fantasy or something that does not exist. Eventually, you start to believe this information as fact, that dreaming is not a reality. For the last five hundred years or so, dreaming has very much been viewed as useless; it is just something you do each night between "real life." But it has not always been this way. In fact, it used to be very different!

Dreaming is something that has been embraced a lot more in history than it is now. Dreaming is taken for granted in the modern world, mostly because of people's lack of understanding, and the knowledge behind why we dream having been lost and/or forgotten. Ancient civilizations had a great understanding of why we dream, and they used to revolve their everyday lives around what they would see in their dreams. In fact, it was very important in helping them function. Dreams were found recorded on clay tablets dating back to around 4000—3000 BC. Ancient civilizations didn't see dreaming as just something you do while you sleep, they actually saw it as an extension of our reality. They didn't seem to try and separate the differences between real life and dreaming but instead molded them together as one and lived their lives this way. Romans and Greeks are great examples on how big of an impact dreams had on their lives. They believed that dreams were direct messages from the Gods forewarning them about future events, or advice and guidance of what they should do. It was seen as a religious morale to listen to your dreams and was highly encouraged. They would not only listen to their dreams, but they would look at them as guidance. They would look into their dreams for answers to problems they were having. For example, before technology was invented to help diagnose a sickness, or help determine what medicine you should take, people would instead look to their dreams for answers on what was wrong with them, and how to heal themselves.

There were also dream analysts that people could go to if they didn't understand their dreams. The dream analysts would analyze the dream for you and give you the messages behind your dreams. Dream analysts were looked up to and highly respected. They were usually a big part of the decision making process for the government or the military. Military leaders would use them to help with tactics in order to defeat their enemies. In the Hellenistic times in Greece, they built temples called Asclepieions, where sick people would go and sleep, and the cures would be given to them via dreams.

Ancient Chinese and Mexican civilizations believed that your spirit would actually leave your body while you were dreaming and it would wander to other places. They believed that if you were to awaken while your body was in a deep sleep, and your spirit was wandering, that it would not find its way back to the body, therefore, you would die. Some cultures still look down upon alarm clocks, for fear of suddenly being woken up. They also believed they were able to speak to their ancestors through their dreams, and that their ancestors were made up of different objects or parts of nature in the dreams, but their spirit was in them. As you can see, dreams had a huge impact on people's lives back in history, and many of them had the same theory of being guided and warned of events in the waking life. However, dreaming was not always looked at as something positive. During the middle ages people looked at dreams as horrible tricks. People believed that while you where dreaming, the devil was tempting you with certain images and temptations in your most vulnerable state. Therefore, they did not embrace dreams, and basically had the exact opposite understanding of them than more ancient civilizations. Now, when you get into more modern times, scientists started doing tests on the brain and body while you're in a dreaming state and found that there is a lot more brain activity going on than when you're awake.

It seems like now people are so sidetracked by technology and materials that they have lost interest in one of the most amazing abilities that they have. The ability to spiritually align yourself and shift dimensions while being able to maintain a physical existence!

So now that you have a better understand of what dreaming actually is – an extension of your reality – and that it also naturally allows you very easy access into the spirit world, I am going to give you another exercise. I am sure you have heard of this exercise before, it is called dream journaling.

Exercise #2
Dream Journaling

Why dream journaling? Because this is the first step in helping you to remember your dreams, even if you do not think that you dream. Secondly, it will allow you to become more familiar with this "other reality" and the other dimensions that you visit. When you become more aware of these things, and you realize on a waking consciousness level that other realities exist and other experiences with the consciousness are possible, then you activate certain potentials within yourself. It alters electromagnetic connections both within the mind, brain, and even perceptive mechanisms. These things will then bring together reservoirs of energy allowing the waking conscious mind to increase its sensitivity. This allows you to no longer be afraid of other realities, which is a huge step in letting your resistance down in order to develop spirit communication. Lastly, it will help you to learn how to analyze what information you are receiving from the spirit world or your Spirit Guides. You are very susceptible to receiving very valid information during your dream state from your Spirit Guides as you have just learned from our little history lesson.

1) First you should pick a good dream journal and leave it by your bed. Pick something that you like, try not to just throw a few sheets of paper over there, unless that's all you have at the moment. A journal specifically picked to be your dream journal helps to keep everything in order and not be cluttered with other things like shopping lists, etcetera. Also, make sure that you have something to write with. I don't want you searching around for something to write with in the morning.

2) This is very *important*: always write in your dream journal first thing in the morning. You are still in a groggy state when you wake up, and you are still

tapped into your higher consciousness, so this is when you can really get some great information. The later in the day it gets, the foggier the dream becomes and it makes it very hard to remember all of the details.

3) Try to write something in your dream journal every day for two months. Even if it's something short that seems insignificant. The reason for this is, many times writing will jog your memory of other things that happened during the dream state. It is also during these two months that you are honing in this new skill.

4) Ask for guidance before you fall asleep. Talk to your Spirit Guide and ask them for their guidance. Ask them to help you with a specific problem at work, a personal issue, or whatever it is that you are stressed about. Do not get frustrated if you do not "dream" your solution right away. This is a training process; you are shifting your perspective on why you dream, and training yourself to utilize dreaming more effectively. This takes time. Your belief system has been in place for many, many years; with the perspective that dreaming was not even useful. This belief has allowed many people to block dreaming from their memory, as insignificant to their life. When you realize it actually is an extension of your reality with the potential to help you to receive much needed guidance, it can also be a little bit of added pressure.

5) Give each dream a name or title. This helps you to find dreams faster if you are searching for a specific one later. It also allows you to sum up the over all "feel" of the experience you are going to be writing down. It's like giving a title to a story. Or in some instances just by naming the dream or giving it a title can trigger an awareness of the overall meaning of the dream.

6) Put more emphasis on the "feel" of the dream than the actual dream itself. Write down symbols and all of that, but make sure you note how you felt through-out the dream; lost, confused, happy, concerned, etcetera. This theme on how you "feel" is repetitive when developing your spirit communication skills. Your sixth sense is felt in the body and throughout this entire process you are going to retrain yourself how to get back in touch with these senses. So, in essence, how you "feel" during the dream is just as important as everything else you can remember.

7) After writing down your dream, look at your dream from an outsider's perspective, like you learned to do during the automatic writing exercise. View it from outside of yourself and try and form an overall picture of what the dream means with no attachment. Try and connect the dots; if you are scared of something and you dream about it, then you are probably facing something during your waking conscious state that

you are scared of. For instance, I used to be scared of tornados, so when I was really stressed out I would dream about them. If I was just a little stressed, I would dream about one or two tornados. However, if I was really stressed out, I would dream about six or seven of them, each one representing something different. When I dream about where I am on my life path, I will dream about roads. Such as where I am on the road, if I am lost on the road, etcetera.

If you do this exercise for a while, slowly you will be able to receive information from your Spirit Guide via dreaming. However, like I mentioned before, be persistent and patient. I worked on this for about a year before I got really, really good at it.

Spirit Guide Communication Meditation

This is a process I strongly recommend, and it seems to be the most popular one, it is a called Spirit Guide Communication Meditation. This is a meditation specifically created and geared towards helping you learn to make contact with your Spirit Guide and help you to become more aware of the sensations or "feelings" when in the presence of your Spirit Guide. This is different than doing a regular meditation, because it has the specific purpose to help you with spirit communication. Here's what you do:

Exercise #3
Spirit Guide Meditation

You can do this lying down on your bed or sitting comfortably in a chair. The best time to do this meditation (unlike your regular meditation) is usually at night before you go to sleep since you won't be interrupted. The veil is also thinner at night and it also helps to prepare you for sleep and interesting dreams.

1) Say a prayer and ask that only the highest vibration of spirits is allowed to make contact with you. Only spirits who come from the white light of the Holy Spirit are allowed in your space. Then see a white light come down from above, see the light surround your body until you are entirely engulfed in the white light. See this white light as a barrier against all other spirits that do not come from the white light of the Holy Spirit.

2) Close your eyes and relax. Relax all of your muscles, starting with your head, your neck, your shoulders, your arms, and your stomach. Feel all of your stress melt away…feel your hips relax, your thighs, your calves and your feet.

3) Imagine you are walking into an elevator and the doors close behind you. You are on the twentieth floor. See the buttons in front of you and push the

button that says one. Feel the elevator begin to move, you are now on your way down. See the numbered display above the elevator doors, and notice that the light has moved from the number twenty to nineteen, as you feel the elevator going down. Continue to watch the lights move to eighteen then seventeen. Breathe deeply between floors. Next you see sixteen and so on. Feel the motion of the elevator as you continue to go down, watch the numbered lights counting down, and count them in your mind as you breathe deeply once or twice between floors. The elevator stops as you reach the first floor, and the doors open. Step out.

4) When you step out there is a path in front of you. This path is a bright yellow path of bricks. On each side of the path is green grass and large beautiful trees. It is sunny outside and there are colorful flowers. You can hear birds in the distance. Step onto the path and follow it along. You reach the bridge and continue across, you can hear the running water below; it is very soothing. Follow the path as it leads you up to a cottage. This cottage has a very beautiful wood door with carvings in it. Look at the craftsmanship and admire its features.

5) When you are ready, go into the cottage, open the door, and walk in. In the middle of the room you will see two chairs, one is for you and one is for your

Spirit Guide. The chairs have a high back and they are facing the other way, so you cannot see who is sitting in the chair. Walk around the chairs and see who is there. What do they look like? Are they male or female? Are they tall or short, dark hair or light hair? Is their hair short or long? How old are they? What are they wearing?

6) Have a conversation with them and ask them what they would like you to know. Then listen. Usually they will communicate with you by blocks of thought via telepathy; however, sometimes you can hear them with your "inner ear." What pictures are you seeing? What words are you seeing? Can you hear anything? Is there anyone else in the room? Do they want to talk with you? If so, ask what messages they have for you. They may also communicate with you by connecting with your claircognizance, and you will just "know" what message they are trying to convey.

7) Spend some time "feeling" what it is like to be in the presence of your Spirit Guide, even if you cannot see them completely. Even if you can just sense their presence, spend some time becoming familiar with how it feels. What sensations are you experiencing? Can you feel them behind you or in front of you? To which side of you do you feel them? Do you feel warm in their presence, or tingly? Do you feel your chakras opening? All of these sensations are

important because you will become accustomed to feeling these sensations when your Spirit Guide is around. In fact, these sensations will begin to help you differentiate when you are thinking of something yourself or when your Spirit Guide is trying to communicate a message to you. When you're receiving spirit communication, they will be accompanied by these sensations. That is how you will be able to tell the difference: if the messages are not accompanied by some type of physical sensation, then it is most likely your own great idea or note to self!

8) When you are done experiencing the presence of your Spirit Guide, thank them and exit the cottage. Make sure to close the door behind you. Follow the yellow brick path back over the bridge and to the elevator. Then step into the elevator and push the button for number twenty. The doors will close and you will begin to feel the elevator moving upward. Watch the numbers rise and light up as you move past the other floors. Floor one, two, three; take a nice deep breath between each floor as you feel the elevator moving up. Four, five, six, and so on until you reach floor twenty. The elevator will stop and the doors will open. Step out and open your eyes. You're done.

Now that you know how to get to your cottage, you can go back there any time and talk to whomever you find there. You can spend some time there and design the cottage in any way you wish. You can add windows, things to write on, furniture; whatever makes you feel comfortable and happy. When you become comfortable with the process, you might want to ask for help with a particular issue before going into the meditation, and see what answers come to you when you get to your cottage. The journey should feel relaxing and enjoyable. Sometimes when you work on developing your spirit communication through avenues such as this, you may even receive the answers in your dream state (which is similar to this meditative state). The insights on this journey are invaluable. The dreams you'll have after doing this exercise may be a little more clear than usual. Pay attention to them and what they might be trying to tell you. Make sure to write them in your dream journal.

Five Common "Blocks"

You have learned a lot about spirit communication as well as many exercises to try. I am confident that you have learned enough to help you with a strong start. In closing, I wanted to address some issues, in case you find yourself running into some hang-ups along the way. So I went ahead and made a list of the most common blocks people encounter when learning to communicate with their Spirit Guide. What do I mean by blocks? It's just like it sounds, a list of five things that can keep you from being able to discover your ability to communicate and work with your Spirit Guide. I have also given solutions for each block, as I want you to have all of the tools that you need to make this a very satisfying journey.

Block #1
You Have Not Been Properly Educated

This one is very, very common. If you do not get enough information on what to look for, what to be aware of, and simply how Spirit Guides communicate with you, it is very hard to filter through all of the different avenues yourself. Even if you do a successful job, without verification, or the proper knowledge of signs to look for to help you verify you are on the right path, you will question yourself and brush it off. What I have noticed from years of teaching is that students who came to me were not getting enough information about how the whole communication process works. There are so many things that you need to be aware of, important things, and many of those were being left out. I am confident that I have covered all of those things here in this book. If I have left something out and you have a question that has not been covered, please go to my website and e-mail me; contact information will be at the end of the book. I will be happy to answer those questions for you.

Block #2
Your Belief System

Your belief system is something which you have spent many years working long and hard at creating; so do not be upset if you cannot seem to break down these barriers overnight. You have probably trained yourself for over ten years to not believe in spirits. Just think about it; every time you "feel" something behind you or get a block of thought from someone who has passed, you immediately brush it off as impossible. When people "feel" a presence, most of the time it scares the daylights out of them so they do whatever they can to not feel the presence anymore. Can anyone say "blocking"? There have been too many scary movies out there portraying the spirit world as evil or scary and something that can harm us (thanks movie industry). If you are not scared you tend to go another route: 'seeing is believing.' People need to be able to "see" things in order to believe in them. If you cannot see something, like spirits, it is hard for you to wrap your mind around the possibility that they are real. To believe that spirits or Spirit Guides actually exist, is quite a magical feeling, because it is quite magical! What have you been told about anything that gives you that magical feel, like Santa Claus, the Tooth Fairy, or the Easter Bunny? Well, you see where I am going with this. It is more important, now than ever, to challenge and restructure your belief system.

Block #3
Your Sensitivity Level Is Low

This directly relates to Block #1 and Block #2, so this will change for you as you have gained the knowledge to raise your sensitivity by reading this book. Again, I know I am repeating myself, but you have spent many years trying not to "feel" spirits. So it is going to take some work to bring yourself "in tune" again. This tuning is a real thing. Imagine it like this: say you were a really good runner when you were young. Now that you are older, you have let yourself get out of shape and you do not run anywhere, you just sit at your desk all day. Then, you heard about a race you would like to attend. It is a couple of months out so you decided to enter. You would need to start taking the proper steps to tone your muscles again and get them prepared for the task ahead. You would need to work on your cardio so it could support your muscles and sustain your body during the duration of the race. Your muscles would not just go out there and perform to the best of their ability because you where asking them to. Just because you used to do it and you are fully capable of doing it. Without the proper training and exercises beforehand to help get you into shape, you would not perform very well. Spirit communication is the same thing, you are fully capable, but in order to do it properly there needs to be training and exercises in order to get yourself "tuned" up and back into shape.

Block #4
You Are Overlooking the Signs

Have you ever heard of the joke about the guy whose house was flooding? This man was at his house when a dam broke and water was coming towards his home, when a fire truck came by and told him, "You need to evacuate, your house is going to go under water."

The man was praying and said, "No thanks, God is going to save me."

The flooding was getting worse and the water had filled up the first floor of his house.

So the man went to the second floor and began praying when a boat came to his window and two police officers said, "You need to come with us, sir, your house is going to go under water soon."

The man turned to them and said, "No thank you, God is going to save me."

So they drove away in their boat to help other people. Then the water began rising to the second floor, so the man climbed onto the roof of the house and was praying, when he spotted a helicopter.

The rescue people yelled at the man through the loud speaker, "Sir, grab onto the ladder. You need to come with us or you are going to drown."

The man looked up and yelled, "No thank you, God is going to save me!"

So the helicopter left and the man drowned. When he got to heaven he was a little upset and said to God, "What happened? I thought you where going to save me?"

God looked at him confused and said, "I sent you a fire truck, a boat, and a helicopter. What more do you want from me?"

People do this often, overlook the obvious signs of help, or obvious answers to a problem they are having, because it is presented in a manner that seems too obvious. Do not limit your perception on the manner in which Spirit Guides will help and guide you. Many times people assume that the solution must be given to them in a complicated, woo woo, kind of way. This is not always the case, the solution might be right in front of you and your guides may have very well had something to do with it!

Block #5
Giving Up Too Soon

Like I mentioned before in Block #3, it takes some time to "tune" yourself in again and it will most likely not happen overnight. You need to be committed to learning how to communicate with your Spirit Guide for a period of at least six months. Don't try it for a couple of days or even weeks and then say, "It's not working!" If that's your plan, I will save you some time here and tell you now, you are right, it probably won't work. Your success depends on knowledge (gained here), practice (what you learned), challenging your beliefs (this part is actually fun and you should do this all the time anyway), being consistent, and being patient. Those things take some time, so do not give up too soon. I have taught thousands of people how to contact their Spirit Guides, and I have a huge success rate. All of this information has been gathered over more than twenty years of teaching and if you follow these things, I have no doubt in my mind that you too, will be successful!

The Pursuit of Happiness

of

Happiness

21 Spiritual Rules To Success

Jennifer O'Neill

Spiritual Rule #1

Understand You Are a Reflection of Your Choices

"Blaming is so much easier than taking responsibility, because if you take responsibility ...then you might be to blame."

I want you to take a moment and give some thought to the people who surround you, the people who are currently in your life right now. Observe them for a minute. It might be a member of your family, friends, or coworkers, whomever you choose. I want you to observe his or her life, with no attachment and no judgment on your part. Now think about it, these people are clearly a reflection of the choices they have made in their life so far. They are in their current situation because of all of the choices they have made in their lifetime, and those choices have helped to contribute to where they are at today. Some of the choices they have made have most likely been good, and some of them no doubt have been bad, but they all had "choices." You are also a reflection of the accumulation of choices that you have made throughout your lifetime. The wonderful and most amazing thing about this is that you do indeed have choices. In fact, you have many choices, every single day. The downside is you must also take responsibility for the choices you make. The ones you have made up until this point, and the ones you continue to make, every single day.

Now, you may wonder, "How does this correlate to my own life exactly?" Well, here are some examples. Were you a teen parent? Did you finish high school or go to college? Did you pursue what it is that you love doing most in life? Or did you settle because that's what everyone else did? Did you marry for love? Did you stay for the kids? These are all choices, and choices that may have very clearly defined your life in some way.

Everyone has issues they need to work through, and even overcome; no one is immune to problems. It doesn't matter who you are, where you work, or if you work, it is something we all have in common as human beings. How we choose to deal with these issues, however, is what sets people apart; that is the difference.

> *"It's not about if you have chaos in your life,*
> *it's about how well you manage it."*

When people are unhappy, they blame many other things. They blame the economy, the government, their health, their spouse or significant other, their parents, their childhood, you name it ... there is definitely something beyond their control causing their unhappiness, because they would not be in their current situation by choice! That would be ridiculous! Or would they?

There are some very successful people in the world who will settle for nothing short of success! They work and they plan, they fail and they overcome, but they will succeed. There are also some people who never seem to be able to get it together. They self-sabotage, they are broke, they are unhappy, and they never (they believe) ever seem to be able to catch a break. They will continue to make choices over and over that will match who they believe they are, because your choices are very much a reflection of your personality.

Take a minute to answer these questions about yourself, truthfully:

1) What do you think other people see when they look at you?
2) Does it reflect your personality?
3) Does it match who you want to be?
4) What choices have you made to contribute to where you are at currently in life?

This is just a series of questions to help you to expand your mind and shift your perspective. You have so many wonderful choices in life; however, many times people do not see it that way. They *choose* to see it another way, the way in which they have no choice. You can look at it this way if you wish, but it is simply not true; you always have a choice, so own up to the choices you make. Now, some of the choices you have made in life may have been good choices, and some of them may have been bad choices, but that really doesn't matter anymore ... what matters is NOW!

How to make choices that work for you:

1) You are no longer a victim; you are a choice maker!

Start seeing yourself that way and take responsibility for the choices you are making from here on out. If you want to lose weight, stop eating unhealthy foods. If you are unhappy, figure out what choices you are making that are contributing to your unhappiness. There are no excuses here; if you don't like what's happening, fix it. If you don't want to fix it, then don't complain about it!

2) Make choices that are in alignment with who you are and where you want to see yourself in the future.

This is very *important!* Stop making choices that are not in alignment with who you are, period! This causes resistance and resentment. It makes you bitter and uncomfortable when you make choices that do not align with who you are, but most people do it anyway. Many times people feel their own discomfort is less important than someone else's comfort. This is trained behavior, drilled into us at a young age. You are considered "selfish" if you put your own comfort or happiness in front of someone else's comfort or happiness. Selfishness is ludicrous! "How dare you not help me feel better first!" That seems a bit hypocritical if you ask me. Especially since it is not possible to make other people happy (see spiritual rule #5), if this is being selfish, by all means, be selfish! Of course, I am not talking about completely ignoring the wants and needs of those around us, or causing someone intentional harm. However, you cannot help someone else who is not willing to help themselves. In order to help those who are willing to help themselves effectively, you must be coming from a place of fulfillment and happiness.

3) Own the power of choice!

Take your head out of the sand! It is time to recognize that you, and you alone, have a tremendous amount of power over who you are. No one else holds this power over you, unless of course, you *choose* to give up this power to him or her. Understand that ultimately you are the final decision maker in your own life. There is no one to blame; you are the CEO in charge!

You can try and figure out how this rule does not apply to you, and you can go about your day feeling sad, depressed, and hopeless. Or you can choose to change what you don't like. The wonderful thing is, it's your choice!

You are never stuck, unless you are choosing to stay there.

You are never limited, unless you choose to limit yourself.

You are never less than, unless you choose to see yourself this way.

You will never fail, unless you choose failure as an option.

You are powerful beyond belief!

Spiritual Rule #2

Do Not Let Your Relationship Status Define Your Happiness

"You cannot borrow half of who you are from someone else, yet people try to do it all of the time, they just call it a relationship!"

This is a very common mistake people make, attaching their happiness to their relationship status. If you are unhappy right now, and say that you don't do this ... well, I don't believe you! You've heard it a million times before, "This is my better half," or "They complete me!" It has become an accepted way of thinking in society today, and it is causing a huge problem. People think it is natural, or common, to feel "whole" when you are in a relationship, in fact, they do not even think twice about it! Society has adapted the mind-set that wholeness and relationships are linked, they have unknowingly blended the two together. The problem is, you cannot borrow half of who you are from someone else, and this is exactly what you are trying to do when you feel this way! As a result, people have become very focused on being in a relationship, because they like the way they *feel* when they are in one. What they don't pay attention to is what they are actually experiencing. Distraction!

"What?" I am sure you are wondering, "How does that work?" Well, it's really pretty easy. Whenever you do not *feel whole* you are experiencing what is called a spiritual void. This spiritual void happens when your soul is being malnourished in a sense. You are not fulfilling yourself on a soul level (in other words, you are breaking many of the rules in this book.) When your soul is malnourished this feeling becomes very noticeable, and many times, it is mistaken for loneliness. How does this involve your relationship? When you are in a relationship, most people no longer notice the void, another person is essentially distracting them. You become more focused on what this other person is doing, and what they are doing now, and now, you get the drift. When another person becomes such a focus in your life, under these circumstances, your happiness meter begins to fluctuate with their behavior. Your happiness then becomes attached to your significant other and your relationship. Of course, it is natural to have things in your relationship affect your happiness from time to time, for a "temporary" time period. In fact, there is no way to avoid it. When you are arguing, or going through a stressful time in your life or in your relationship, your happiness can become affected. What I am talking about here is becoming so focused on your relationship status, that your relationship's effect on your happiness is not temporary, but permanent! Now, I have broken this down into two different categories for you, so here they are:

If You Are In a Relationship

If you are in a relationship and your partner seems to have a HUGE impact on your day-to-day happiness. (Now, I do not expect you to know this if you are one of these people, but your friends will, so ask them.) If your friends constantly complain to you, and say things like, "You will never be happy with so and so," or they are tired of hearing you complain to them about your relationship, there is a problem. Just to reiterate, there will be days when you and your significant other will argue, or whatever, and it will affect your happiness (temporarily), and that is normal. But when you are experiencing a spiritual void and do not feel whole yourself and you do not have anything else going on in your life to focus upon that is good for you, your primary focus *will* become your relationship. Your focus will become your partner and what your partner is doing. Every move they make will give you a mood swing.

If You Are Not In a Relationship

If you are not in a relationship and you only seem to be happy when you are in one, this is a big problem! Yes it is normal to be lonely (to an extent), yes it is normal to want a companion, but it is not ~~normal~~ (it is absurd how many people think this is normal so I *choose* to use a different word here), it is not "healthy" to feel happy only when you are in a relationship. This is in fact a huge red flag that you have a spiritual void going on in your life that you need to fill!

How do you fill spiritual void?

Start with Spiritual Rules #6, #10 and #15 right away!

Spiritual Rule #3

Remove All Contingency Clauses Attached To Your Happiness!

"When working with the Universal Laws you are working with the laws of manifestation, not instant gratification ..."

People have become very spoiled. I would go so far as to say, in many instances, that adults many times behave like spoiled children! As the world has become more materialistic, so have humans. Materialism has begun to overwhelm the physical senses. Materialism is a big contributing factor to people placing contingency clauses on their happiness, and the funny thing is, they do not even know they are doing it unless it is brought to their attention. However, from this day forward, understand since this has now been brought to your attention, you may no longer use this as an excuse!

I hate to break the news to you, but as humans, we are fickle people. As fickle people here is the problem: when one thing on your "I will be happy when list" gets crossed off, another item will promptly take its place, then another, then another, and so on. If you are thinking, "I don't do this!" not so fast. The tricky part here is, most of the people who do this (and it is a lot of people), *do not notice* that they are doing it. Because it is another "accepted" way of thinking by society today, so it has made this thought process very easily disguisable.

Do you do any of these things?

1) Do you think about retiring often and how nice it will be?
2) Are you aggravated at work and often wish you worked somewhere else?
3) Do you wish you lived somewhere else?
4) Do you wish you had a different car, house, etcetera?
5) Do you live beyond your means?
6) Do you wish you were in/out of a relationship often?

If you answer yes to three or more of these questions, you have most likely adapted very well to this thought process. Most likely, without knowing it, you have probably been placing contingency clauses on your happiness.

What contingency clauses have you knowingly or unknowingly placed on your happiness?

Now that this has been brought to your attention, I want you to think about this question for a minute. Here are some examples to help get you started: When I get out of this place, I will be happy. When I get a better job, I will be happy. When I can retire, I will be happy. When I can purchase XYZ, I will be happy. Try and think of as many contingency clauses you have placed (knowingly or unknowingly) on your happiness, as you can. Why?

Because it raises your awareness … and awareness is key to changing this behavior!

When you become more aware of this type of thinking it becomes a habit that you can easily break. But most likely you may not have been aware of it until now. You may also be surprised at how often you find yourself, or other people, thinking this way. When you remove contingency clauses attached to your happiness, it will force your attention into "the now" and finding joy today. This simple action is helping you to find happiness within the life you have already created, your life as it is today, not your life as you hope it will be tomorrow.

Spiritual Rule #4

Release Yourself From Expectations

"Do you see the people in your life for who they really are, or do you see them how you want them to be? Never keep someone in your life because you are expecting them to change, keep them in your life because you appreciate them regardless of change!"

An expectation is a *belief* that there will be a certain outcome in the future, which may or may not be realistic. A *belief* is when you have faith or confidence, that something is fact or true, without substantial proof. Expectations usually involve another person, or people, or an outcome of a situation, oftentimes resulting in disappointment.

Wow! I bet you never realized how complicated having an expectation could be. Expectations are extremely toxic to your happiness!

Problems with expectations:

#1 Element of control

When people have placed an expectation on someone or something, it is usually because they want to *control* what the outcome essentially is. When an expectation is placed, there is *resistance* to any other outcome than what is "expected." You have decided this is the only acceptable outcome (otherwise, there would be no expectation.)

#2 Belief

Belief means that you "believe" there will be a certain outcome in the future, which may or may not be realistic, without substantial proof! The crazy thing about this is you have no substantial proof that things are going to turn out the way you expect them to, yet you are still "expecting" it to turn out the way in which you "believe" it will. One of the greatest things about the future is that the future is constantly changing. However, that also makes it hard to anticipate a certain outcome.

#3 Disappointment

When you become rigid in your thinking, you have a very high probability of disappointment. The act of feeling disappointment itself is not the whole problem, but the resistance that you feel in the body as a result of acquiring an expectation is. Resistance and other negative feelings felt energetically in the body, such as disappointment, can and do cause illness.

Releasing yourself from expectations:

1) Release yourself from your own expectations.

This is going to be hard for many people and yet one of the most freeing things that you will ever experience. Stop expecting others to behave differently! Why? *Because you cannot control other people's behavior!* Period! I don't care how hard you try, the illusion that you can control another person's behavior is just that, an illusion. I don't care if the other person is two years old or eighty-two years old, they choose to react to you, or a situation, all on their own. Now you can "wish" they behave differently, but do not expect it. The best thing you can do for yourself is to accept other people's behavior and the choices they make. You may not agree with them, you may even wish them to do things differently, but accept it. Just as you would appreciate other people accepting the choices that you make.

2) Release yourself from expectations that other people put on you.

All people put expectations on someone or something in order to reduce the anxiety, fear, or worry that they have within themselves. They want to feel calm inside, and in order to do that, many people "mistakenly" think that the calmness comes from outside of themselves. So they do their best to control their environment. The problem with this is that you may be "in their environment." So do not alter what is best for you in order to calm someone else's environment. Because you do not have that much control over their environment!

"Control is an illusion. You will never be able to control anything, any situation, or anyone without consent. So in actuality there is no control, there is only consent!"

Spiritual Rule #5

Do Not Hold Anyone Else Responsible For Your Happiness

"You would not want to be responsible for someone else's happiness, so please do not hold someone else responsible for yours!"

This is going to be a challenge for many people! But the challenge is not without its rewards!

Today I would like you to commit to taking COMPLETE responsibility for your own happiness!!!

I bet some of you are almost laughing thinking, "Are you kidding? That's it? This will be easy." Well good, then you should welcome the challenge!

How relieved would you feel if you knew that no one, and I mean no one, could affect your happiness? Your happiness was perfectly preserved inside of yourself, protected from all of the negativity that flourishes in the world outside of yourself. Not a single soul could taint your happiness, not your spouse, not your kids, your parents, or your boss, no one! Just bask in that feeling for a minute ... doesn't it feel nice? Don't you almost feel lighter knowing that other people cannot affect your happiness? Well, this might be your lucky day because this is reality. Most likely, up until this point your perception has probably been different, that your happiness is vulnerable. You see, people react to other people all day long; you react to someone's tone of voice, their facial expressions, their body language, etcetera. You even react to situations that you are in, so a large portion of your day is actually spent reacting to other people's behaviors. Reaction should not define your happiness, and it is really energy wasted. You might be thinking, "I am not into drama, I don't do this. But I know people who do." Well let me assure you, everyone does this! The key here is to be aware of it, and keep your reactions to other people's thoughts and actions in perspective. I have put together some steps for you to try and keep things in perspective.

1) Meditation/Visualization

I like to start my day with a visualization technique. It is kind of like a mini meditation, and I would like you to try it. You start out by finding a comfortable chair to sit in, and relax your body completely. However, instead of going into a deep meditation, I want you to spend some time visualizing your day. In order to utilize this visualization technique at its most effective level, I do not want you to visualize how the day's events are going to go, only concentrate on visualizing yourself and how you feel at the end of the day. See yourself feeling wonderful and satisfied on how the day's events unfolded. Do not go over any particulars, only concentrate on the happy, satisfied "feeling" that you are experiencing. Imagine yourself reflecting on your day after dinner and saying to yourself, "What a great day!" *It is important not go over any details*, just concentrate on how you feel at the end of the day. Imagine that you feel lighter, and happy about the daily events. Do this in the morning.

2) Release Expectations

Since we just went over this in chapter four, you should have a good handle on how this works. Today I want you to throw all of the expectations that you have placed on others out the window. You may not punish anyone, by anger, the silent treatment, or whatever, for not living up to expectations that YOU have set for them. Expectations are way too common and you definitely set yourself up for disappointment when you have them. The funny thing is, most of the time people do not even tell other people what their expectations are of them! They just take for granted that there are a lot of mind readers out there. Now that is definitely setting someone up to fail!

3) Stop Taking Things So Personally

For today, keep your emotions in check by not reacting negatively, or responding in anger, to someone else having a bad day. People who are having a bad day like to spread it around and you may be in the crossfire! Do not *allow* them to affect your happiness. Even if you feel that it is directed at you (usually it is because you are at the wrong place at the wrong time.) Who cares if they are unhappy, it's not your problem, "Do not take someone else's unhappiness personally."

4) Stop Being Resentful

Do not force yourself to do the things you hate, and then resent doing it the whole time. If you are working at a job you hate, it's not anyone else's fault, you have free will, and it's a choice. So as long as you are staying at a job, or doing laundry, shift your perspective and be happy that you have free will. Be happy that you are healthy, be happy that you have a job, or laundry to do, etcetera. No one can force you to do something without your "free will consent"! So stop being bitter about it!

5) No Drama

DO NOT engage in any drama and/or judge anyone and their situation. This is about your happiness, not about how you can fix other people's happiness!

6) Boycott the News

Do not watch the news or read the newspaper. Those events are 98 percent negative and out of the realm of your control. If the world is coming to an end, a hurricane is coming, or the gas prices are going up, I promise you, someone will tell you about it.

Spiritual Rule #6

Pursue At Least One
of Your Dreams

*"When you follow your dream, life is easy.
When you follow someone else's dream,
life is unsatisfying. When you forget to
dream, life is just plain confusing!"*

This is important, so listen up! When you are pursuing at least one of your dreams, it will resonate with you on a soul level. When this happens you will begin to offer a different vibration, energetically, out into the Universe. Why does that matter? Because you are magnetized! Think of it this way, think of yourself as a human magnet. As a human magnet, the higher you vibrate the more powerful of a magnet you become, the lower you vibrate, the less powerful of a magnet you become. You begin to work with the Laws of Attraction, when your magnet is powerful, and things will begin to fall into place. Life gets easier, opportunities will begin to present themselves to you, it is amazing! Plus, let's face it, it's just fun! Please don't make excuses that you do not have time to pursue any of your dreams; it has been reported that people spend an average of eight hours a month on Facebook; use that time!

Here is an example:

I get asked a lot, "How did you end up in Hawaii?"
I say, "We sold everything we owned and we moved here!"
Other person, "Wow, I could never do that! But I sure would like to!"
"Why?"
"Why what?"
"Why couldn't you do that?"
Then comes the puzzled look, "Because I have a mortgage, a job, family, etcetera, etcetera ..."

You can always come up with a hundred excuses of why you cannot to do something, in fact, people think of excuses all the time! Why they can't move somewhere, why they can't change jobs, can't travel, or even relax. "There are too many things I need to get done!" I swear people's motto is, "I can't because ..." Let's be honest, people only make excuses to justify staying where they are at in life, or in a situation that they hate. They do it so they can feel better about not going after their dream, like somehow justifying it makes it acceptable. They make excuses because if they don't, everyone around them will tell them what a bad idea following their dream is! That's right, they will, and they did it to us too! If you are wondering, here is how we followed one of our dreams.

My husband and I decided that we needed to make a change. We had two houses and a construction company. The economy in the town where we lived began to get worse, and this was affecting the construction industry. Then my husband began experiencing heart pains. (Heart attacks happen when you are living a life that you no longer enjoy or you are stressed out all the time, in fact, it is quite common.) So my husband asked, "How about we move to Hawaii?" We discussed it and booked him a ticket. He left a week later to see what he thought and if we should move there. He made an appointment with a realtor and looked at housing in different neighborhoods. He also checked out job opportunities and talked with the local people he met along the way. When he came home he said, "Let's move!"

So we started filtering through all of our things, and had an auction (it is amazing to me how little you get for material items, after paying so much for them in the first place). That is definitely when my whole view on material things changed! We had so much stuff! Things we never used or had forgotten we had. We put both houses on the market and then we told family and friends. Oh jeez, they thought we had lost it! It's way too expensive there, what about jobs, what about the cost of living, what about us? Everyone was convinced that groceries were higher, gas was higher, housing was higher and they had state income tax! I was surprised at how many things they thought of, I was surprised at the fear! But we were not afraid, and we had moved within two months. We had no furniture, no jobs, but we were in Hawaii!

Over the next three months we found jobs, we found furniture, and we made more money than before. Housing was higher, gas was higher, food was about the same, but clothes and car insurance were way cheaper. The pay was higher, and the law requires that all employers provide you with health insurance. All in all we are financially better off and my husband's cholesterol went from three hundred to under two hundred! There was a downside, however; you are a six-hour plane ride away from the mainland, no more road trips! Family was now far away, and it is expensive to fly back and forth. In fact, moving to Hawaii isn't for everyone; it does take some serious adjustment.

Stop being afraid to follow your dreams. Stop being afraid to make a big change! Stop letting material things tie you down, financially or geographically.

It is the most incredible feeling after so many years of having multiple houses, cars, and things, to just free yourself, so that you can go anywhere or do anything you want. I love the freedom and I will never collect that much stuff again. The crazy thing is after you move five thousand miles away from your previous home of thirty some odd years, to an island, you really conquer your fear! For the first couple of months I would think to myself, "What did we do?" But I adjusted to the initial shock that can sometimes follow change and I began to feel different, I began to feel like, "I can do anything, I can move anywhere. I am adaptable!"

Pursuing one of your dreams does not have to be a big move. For you it might be something like skydiving, taking a trip to Europe, going on a plane ride, or a roller coaster ride, enrolling in a Zumba class, learning French, visiting a friend, going to a spa, eating sushi, or volunteering at a homeless shelter.

Today I want you to make a plan to do something that you have wanted to do for a while, but you have not yet done, due to lack of money, lack of time, fear, family, whatever! I want you to check an item off of your "Bucket List" so to speak! People spend a lot of time and energy talking themselves out of doing something, or even planning to do something that they have always wanted to do. The reasons are endless! I don't have time, my kids are little, I don't have money, I will do that when I retire. Nope, you are going to "plan" it right now!

Dream time!

1) Pick something you have wanted to do for a while. Something that you are really excited about, or passionate about, something that you have made many excuses not to do, until now.

2) Set a date to start, to enroll, or try this new thing. The date cannot be longer than a year from today, unless it is a trip to Europe or around the world. But DO NOT set the date longer than five years out!

3) If money is an issue, find a jar, a piggy bank, or an empty bottle and label it. Put all of your change in the jar, everyday. Then, if you can, put the same amount of money in the jar every payday, five dollars, ten dollars, or fifty dollars, whatever you are comfortable with. You can even sell things, have a rummage sale, or pick up some extra hours at work, but make funding your excursion a fun focus.

4) Excuses are null and void here, they do not apply, and it is your mission to make this thing happen. It is not your mission to name a million reasons why it won't or can't happen, because we already know that you can do that just fine! This is a mission to overcome limits that you have set for yourself.

The purpose of this exercise is to help you to begin to restructure your old belief system.

This is not just a self-indulgent moment or exercise. Our belief system is what keeps us limited. When your belief system is supported by "I can't," or "It's just the way it is," it will affect aspects of your life that you are not even aware of. This is a pattern, and a way of life for many people, *it is learned behavior, not the way life works!* This exercise is designed to help your confidence grow. Experiences like this help you to become spiritually rich. You never hear people when they get older say, "I wish I would have accumulated more stuff!" They do, however, many times, regret not experiencing more of the things that life had to offer.

Spiritual Rule #7

Stop Looking For Happiness In the Future and Learn to Experience Happiness In the Present!

"Enjoy the moment. Everyone has become so busy looking ahead and worrying about their future, and looking at yesterday to see what went wrong, that they are forgetting to enjoy today."

When you are looking to the future for happiness, it means that you are failing to find it today. A lot of times this is an indication that bigger and better things are now defining your happiness. In other words, you have become "desensitized" to the little joys in life. Things like birthday parties, having lunch with a friend, enjoying the weather, laughing, or hearing someone laugh. When you are constantly looking towards the future to find happiness that is where your focus also lies; your thoughts become occupied by what lies ahead. The "now" becomes insignificant.

Experiencing happiness in the present requires:

1) Being more present!

Simply being more present and aware of what is happening around you at the time can open you to experiencing more happiness. People find it really hard to be present a lot of the time. They come home from work and they are preoccupied with thoughts of the day's events, or preoccupied with what it is they have to do tomorrow, or on the weekend. They rush to make dinner, all the while planning the future; who picks up whom, what chore needs done, what needs to be prepared for tomorrow, and so on. The next thing you know, today is yesterday and you weren't present at either place! Talk to your kids or spouse while looking "at" them. Not while you are looking at the stove, or at the computer, but by actually acknowledging their presence. They are your family and they deserve this from you. Observe what is going on around you, in your actual "physical" space, not your mental space, or your cyber space.

2) Have some down time.

Make a certain time during the day in which you have "down time." A good time to do this is during the evening when everyone is home. It should be consistent, so that your family and friends know there will be a time when you are approachable and mentally present for them if needed. Down time is the time in which you unplug, do no work, or planning of the future. All family events, lunches, or dinners should be included in down time!

3) Unplug!

Put your cell phone and your computer away, and truly engage with others around you. Electronic devices are in full force trying to take over the world, and we appreciate that, but there is a time and place for everything. *It is important for you to unplug at some point during the day, every day, if you want to keep yourself present in the real world.*

4) Make lists for mental clutter.

This is a great way to help keep yourself in the present. People all have mental clutter. What is mental clutter? All of the things that you juggle around in your thoughts, in order not to forget things that need to get done, or things that need to be addressed at some point in the future. Instead of keeping them active in your thoughts, release yourself of the responsibility of remembering them by putting those thoughts down on paper. Then, make a habit of addressing them each morning. When you do this it allows you to free your mind, freeing it from the responsibility of being tied up with all of that information until morning. This allows your mind to relax into the present much easier, with much less multitasking to do.

Experiencing happiness in the present requires you to be present *mentally*! As you get older you will never remember that phone call you had to take, or the Facebook message you needed to answer, the email you had to answer, or what you were surfing for on the Internet. You will, however, remember the joke that someone told that made you laugh so hard, soda came out your nose.

Spiritual Rule #8

Negative Thinking Is Contagious...

*"Negative thinking is contagious, do not infect
yourself with other people's thinking ..."*

People worry all of the time about catching the flu, colds,
or whatever big thing is going around that year. They
don't want to be temporarily down and out, or inconve-
nienced with being physically "sick." Plus, they don't like
the way it feels, and who can blame them? Since it worries them so much, they take proper precautions. They
stay away from people who might be "contagious," they
wash their hands and get flu shots. All the while they are
preoccupied with all of these contagious things, they are
letting one of the most "contagious" things, even more
dangerous to your system, slip right under their radar.
Negative thinking!

"What?" You might think, "Who cares! We are talking about my health here!" Well, you should care, that's for sure. Did you know that around 70 percent of the population are pessimistic thinkers, and that's just a fancy way of saying negative thinkers? Did you know that negative thinking has a *huge* impact on your physical and spiritual health? Did you know that it also has an impact on your money flow, and your life path? I bet the money part got your attention! Well it's true. Do you ever notice how you can be in a great mood, and someone else can come along and ruin your day because of their attitude? Then, the next thing you know you're ruining someone else's day? (Well you probably don't notice the last part.) Well it happens and it happens a lot! Why should you care? Because all of this negative thinking will have an impact in your life and on your health, and that's a fact!

What should you do about it? You can be more aware of how contagious negative thinking is. You can allow yourself not to be swayed by others, and not allow yourself to think everything is going to turn out crappy like they do.

You can stop watching the news!

Anyone else tired of consistently hearing negative things every single time that you turn on the news or open a newspaper? That is exactly why for the past ten years I have boycotted the news. But every once in awhile, I get a glimpse of it and it is an instant reminder of why I boycotted it in the first place! Government Shutdown, The Dow Plunges, More Deaths In Iraq, Bailout Money Where Did It Go? Tired of hearing it!

Now there are natural disasters that do occur, and those things are important to know about, because many of us have family and friends in various places. Even if you do not watch the news you will hear about those things, because somebody will insist on telling you about them. When people find out that I refuse to watch the news or read about it on the Internet, they say, "How are you going to know if anything bad happens?"

"Well," I say, "I can safely assume that according to the news, something bad is happening somewhere in the world, every minute, of everyday. If a tsunami is headed my way, well, we have a very good warning system!" (That warning system consists of alarms going off and fire trucks driving down the street yelling with a loudspeaker system to evacuate, which will wake you out of a dead sleep! See, no need for the news!)

With anything else that seems to be important, I can also safely assume that someone will tell me about it, and believe me they do. It is funny how many people feel the need to tell me the news, or any other bad thing they have heard that is now happening in the world, or with the economy. People I know, and people I don't know, it is a topic of discussion with everybody. Many conversations tend to revolve around all of the scary stuff that is happening out there in the world. People feel it is important, and you must know about it, and they also feel it is important to discuss. The funny thing is, if they had never told me about all of the "bad" things happening out there over the last ten years, my life would be exactly the same! Except for the fact that I would have many precious hours of my life back that would have seen relaxation, instead of having them wasted on all the stress that it caused me at that time.

So why should you stop watching the news? Because for the most part, it is wrapping you up in a tornado of negativity that is unnecessary. It is causing your own perspective to be tainted with hopelessness, fear, and negativity, and this will most definitely affect your life, and not for the better. You see, the news has gotten completely out of control, especially with the Internet. The news is now more utilized as a scare tactic, and as a way to influence the way people think. With anything from health scares (swine flu, bird flu, or influenza A), to the economy, to your safety, and how you should be so afraid of losing money, that you will agree with any solution placed in front of you (government bailout, Iraq war, etcetera) to make those feelings go away. Fear has been used as a form of manipulation for centuries; it is a very powerful and effective swaying tool. Especially when you can instill it into the masses, and what better way to do it than the Internet. Why the Internet? Because it is global, and you can reach many more people that way!

There are many positive things that happen in the world everyday, but who cares about that! Positive stories, they don't sell well, and they don't get your attention. Fear and destruction, now that gets your attention! From being subjected to constant negativity, people have become conditioned, without even knowing it, to be in a consistent state of fight or flight mode, they search for things that they have to protect themselves from. Isn't that sad? Negativity is so present around everyone's lives anymore, that it is considered common. It is more believable anyway; after all, we are surrounded by it every single day. What is the new flu this year? (Because every year the flu mutates into something different, which means more flu shots!) Am I going to lose more money? Is there going to be another war? Is it safe in that country? What about the terrorists? Is the economy going to collapse?

Your focus has an effect on your energetic system and whatever you focus upon will become more present in your life. The more you subject yourself to negativity, the more sensitive you become to it, and the world is a much scarier place. When you insulate yourself from unnecessary fear tactics, the world is not so scary, and life is not so scary. I have other things, during the day, that I would much rather focus my energy upon in my own life. I would much rather spend my spare time laughing, talking with my family, pursuing my dreams, and enjoying Mother Nature! Watch CNN? Please, I will have to pass and I suggest you do too!

Spiritual Rule #9

Do Not Take Other People's Unhappiness Personally

"Unhappiness can be like a virus spreading from one person, to the next person, to the next one, and so on. When someone is mean or rude to you, do not let their unhappiness infect your own life. If you are the unhappy one, please quarantine yourself so you do not infect others!"

Self-esteem for many people is determined by what other people think of them. It all seems to be tied together. Would you like everyone to like you? I am sure many of you would answer, "Yes!" Well good luck with that, because let's face it, no matter how likable you are, getting everyone to like you is next to impossible. You never want this to be a determining factor of how you *feel* about yourself. Why? People may like you today, you may tick them off tomorrow and many times you don't even know what you did, but hormones or hunger could certainly be involved. Because people change their minds like they change their underwear and here is what I mean.

Have you ever really thought about how people form their opinions? You need to look at it this way:

1) People tend to form strong opinions based on their mood at the time.

If they are happy their opinion is more on the positive side. If they are unhappy their opinion is more on the negative side. Just think about it. It is uncommon to hear someone who is in a great mood talk negatively about other people. However, if someone is in a bad mood, look out! They could find something wrong with Mother Teresa if they wanted to. They can lash out at anybody, or anything, without even being provoked and many times they will!

2) People's mood is usually derived from the way their day went, and there are way too many factors that determine someone's day.

For instance, perception, eating, weather, stress, hormones, money, all of these things can have an impact on someone's day. This is pretty self-explanatory, just look at how your day went today. What determining factors played a role in how your day is going, or had an impact on the mood you are in right now?

3) Do you really want how someone else's day went to spill over into your world?

Or have *any* kind of impact on your life for that matter? Um … I don't know about you, but for me that would be a big fat NO! People are way to wishy washy with their opinions about other people, and many times the people who feel the need to make it known what they think about you in the first place, are usually people who are not exactly in a position to be throwing stones.

We all have faults and flaws, that's just life! No one is superior and no one is immune to making bad choices. It is how you learn and grow from all of these different experiences, that is what life is all about. So the next time you hear what someone says about you, don't take it so personally. Change your view, and instead of taking it to heart and letting it spill over into your world, it should give you a little bit of insight into their world and you can think to yourself, "Well I know how your day is going!"

Spiritual Rule #10

Implement Change

"Things will never change if you never plan on changing them. Change requires action, action requires a plan, planning requires thought, and thought changes everything..."

Many times people have things in their life that they would like to change, yet instead of acknowledging what these things are, and fixing them, they silently stew. This stewing is in the back of their head most of the time, on a subconscious level, and stewing builds aggravation.

Changing little things in your life seems so easy, so why do you not do it? Well, because deep down you know the truth, and the truth is that it is not easy at all, in fact, it takes a bit of work.

1) You must first acknowledge that change is needed.

In order to acknowledge that change is needed, you must take responsibility. That alone can make you cringe; for most people this is very hard to do.

2) Then, there is problem solving.

Here is what I am sure many of you are thinking, "What! I do enough problem solving! I problem solve for everybody, my kids, my boss, I am tired of problem solving! I want to watch TV!"

3) Last but not least, you need to believe that your life is worth the work!

This is where it can get tricky. It is funny how much time and energy you can put into helping other people solve their problems, but when it comes to your own life, settling is just easier sometimes than initiating change. Change is not easy, but it is rewarding, and you have to want change more than you want to settle!

So here is a simple way to implement change:

1) Make a list: Make a list of five things that you would like to change in your life. Things like your job, your money situation, car, wardrobe, computer, shoes, a weight issue, hair, etcetera.

2) Write it on paper: Take five sheets of paper and at the top of each page, write one of the five things that you would like to change.

3) Address each piece of paper (or each issue): Under each heading you are going to give some thought to what it is that would help you resolve each issue, or change it for the better. For instance, say your weight is on page one, something that might make you feel better is losing twenty-five pounds, or maybe just looking physically fit, or more tone. If your wardrobe is page two and something you would like to see changed, something that might make you feel better is having updated clothes, or clothes that fit, or clothes that flatter your figure. If your job is on page three, what is it that you want? Do you want more flexibility, more money, a vacation, health insurance, to work closer to home? Be specific. You get the idea.

4) Make a game plan: Make a game plan to clear out the past and bring in the new. If your weight is an issue, part of your game plan could be getting a gym membership, or buying healthier food, or maybe running. *Change does not come about unless initiated!* If you are the one wanting change, and stewing, then you are the one that is going to need to be proactive. You can sit on the couch all you want and visualize losing weight, finding your soul mate, or working somewhere you love, but I guarantee that it will be coupled with the feeling of aggravation, and that is self sabotage at its best! When you have a game plan,

you begin to move towards being proactive, and you will begin to feel an *energetic shift*. This energetic shift is of great importance; **your intent shifts your energy,** and what it is you are projecting out into the Universe. This little shift is a major component to implementing change into your life.

5) Problem solve: Treat each item on your list as if your boss has given you a task to complete, and the task is to resolve each problem to the best of your ability. People can problem solve easier if they are asked to do it by someone else, for someone else's benefit. Write down steps you should take in order to get the results you want, as if you have to show your "game plane" to another person. Or even better, do this with a friend and do show it to another person!

6) Set a date: Put a date under each item of when you plan to start implementing change and moving toward your goal. You can use different dates and work on a different issue each week, or you can work on them all at one time, however you choose.

7) **Note your progress:** this is very important! Because many times people will do several things to initiate change and only remember a handful of them. If you note all of the things that you do, it is like giving your self a pat on the back upon your review. Review your progress at the end of the month!

Spiritual Rule #11

Don't Let Fear Bully You

"If we lived in a world with no fear, then you would never discover the courage you have within."

Most people are really afraid of failure. So afraid, in fact, that it stands in their way of success. You might be thinking. "Failure of what?" Simple, everything! Failing in their relationship, failing in their marriage, failing at their job, failing to find happiness, failing in business, failing their kids, failing their parents, need I go on? People are so afraid of putting themselves out there because if they fail, the feeling is terrible, and sometimes that feeling can be hard to overcome. So it's just avoided all together, no failure, no terrible feeling.

Or if you do seem to gather up the courage to face your fears, everyone will promptly remind you that your chances of failure are HUGE! (Don't you love that?) The divorce rate is soaring, the economy is failing, the world is unstable, and governments are fighting, your chances of being successful are very limited. Then they follow up with, "Are you sure?" with a very concerned look on their face. As if you have just snatched up your sword and are heading out to slay a towering thirty-foot, fire-breathing dragon! (We will name the dragon "FEAR" for the sake of this chapter.) This dragon is very successful; in fact, "FEAR" has won all of its battles thus far. Suddenly you become terrified, "What if I do fail? All of those things are true, so true that no one else is being so brave." You think, "Maybe I shouldn't even bother in the first place? I changed my mind, I better go with the safer choice."

The problem with thinking this way is that *we as spiritual beings were created to experience*; we are built as natural explorers on a soul level. We want to live and we want to experience! So if you never put yourself out there, you are left with a spiritual void, a longing and unsatisfied feeling on a much deeper level, much deeper than you ever even think about.

Everyone is afraid of failing, but for some people, the desire to succeed far outweighs the fear.

That is really what sets many successful people apart from the not so successful people. It is not that they had no fear; it was that *their desire to succeed overpowered their fear of failing.* Here is an example of some famous failures:

1) Michael Jordan – Cut from his high school basketball team (bet they feel pretty stupid).

2) Walt Disney – He was fired by the editor of a newspaper for lacking in ideas. (Good thing that happened or no Disney. That would be weird).

3) Babe Ruth – Struck out 1,330 times.

4) Steven Spielberg – Applied to USC film school, but was rejected three separate times.

5) Donald Trump – Filed bankruptcy three times.

Those are just famous failures with good outcomes, but there are many, many ordinary people (I am sure many people who you know yourself) who have overcome their failures, and their fears, to become very successful in whatever it was they wanted to accomplish. It is important for you to know that most people are scared, they are scared of failing, but the people who overcome those fears and "jump off the high dive" so to speak, experience life the way it is meant to be lived. They feel a satisfaction of trying, down to their very soul. Even if they fail, they learn from that experience and usually will want to try it again. They begin to use any failures as learning material, as knowledge, in order to help them succeed.

"I've missed more than nine thousand shots in my career, I've lost almost three hundred games. Twenty-six times I've been trusted to take the game winning shot and missed. I've failed over and over and over in my life. And that's why I succeed!" – Michael Jordan

Spiritual Rule #12

Worry Less

"Worry less, enjoy more, because more often than not, things will work out anyway."

People worry way too much. The thing with worry is it doesn't change anything … or does it? Your reality is your perception, and your perception is formed by thoughts, beliefs, and experience. *Worry is a thought or concern based on fear that is accompanied by negative emotions.* These emotions accompany the thoughts and images in the mind, and are strongly felt in the body, forming the perfect storm of "worry."

Why should that all matter? Because of these two things:

1) Worry is generally a "concern" of an outcome of a situation that is not based on fact, and backed with

no substantial proof that the outcome will indeed be negative. Your mind then goes straight to what you don't want to happen (with no evidence that it will) and manipulates your thoughts to see how this negative event is a possibility.

2) The more you worry, the more the worry will solidify itself in your mind as a belief or fact.

Worry is based on fear.

People spend far more time thinking about every negative scenario that can happen to them or in their lifetime than they ever spend on a positive scenario that could possibly happen. In fact, negative thinking outnumbers positive thinking two to one, and most of the time it is a much higher ratio. Why? Because, it is easier (or more believable) for people to accept a negative outcome as a possibility than it is for them to accept a positive outcome as a possibility. Isn't that sad? Sad but true.

Worry is being too rigid in your thought pattern.

Worry is believing that there are limited outcomes to any given situation, and you spend most of your time focused on the worst possible outcome. Let the truth be told here, there are so many variables to every outcome that it would be mind boggling if you actually sat down and played out every scenario in your head.

Worry is based on negative thought and thoughts do become your reality.

Thoughts are energetic wave patterns that are sent out into the Universe and the wave patterns actually come together to form, and to become things. The energetic wave patterns of thoughts can be measured; this is quantum physics not metaphysics. Your thoughts go out into the Universe, and form your reality, *if you are not resistant to it*. In other words, if you can "feel" that it is a possibility, it is. When you worry, not only do you "feel" that the negative outcome is a possibility, the more you worry the more you obsess about it becoming your reality, the more energy you are focusing towards a potentially negative outcome. Then when it happens you say, "I knew this would happen, this is why I worry!" There, now you have more proof to justify your worrying for next time.

Worry is normal to an extent.

Worry is a normal emotion; in fact, everybody has experienced worry in his or her lifetime. It is okay to worry now and again as long as you do not obsess about whatever made you worry in the first place. Because more often than not, things will work themselves out. However, it is important when you allow worry into your thoughts, that you also allow worry to leave without forcing the worry to "park" itself there. It is unrealistic to never worry about anything, worry will happen on occasion and that's okay. Just do not allow worry to come into your thoughts and hang out and loiter around, kick the worry out and occupy your thoughts with something else.

Break yourself of the habit of worrying.

People only seem to remember all of the times they worried that resulted in things turning out badly, just as they expected them to. Then they pocket that experience for a later date in order to justify more worrying. People very conveniently forget about all of the other times that their worry was unfounded. Here is a good trick to break yourself of this habit:

1) Take a piece of paper and write down every thing you are worried about right now. Anything you are worrying about, bills, school, a relationship, do not skimp here, write it all down.

2) Then seal this in an envelope and put it somewhere you will remember with a date to be opened in three months.

3) In three months when you open the envelope, you will most likely be surprised at all of the things you were worried about that turned out just fine. You will also probably have forgotten about many of the things that you put on the list. This trick is a good way to show yourself how things mostly do work out in your favor.

Spiritual Rule #13

Let It Go...

"Many times people find it very hard to break attachments! If something is not working after reasonable effort ... LET IT GO! When you are focusing your energy towards something that is not manifesting, it is "stuck," or hung up somewhere. Letting things go can be exhilarating! On an energetic level you will feel a lot lighter, because tension and resistance is then released."

Letting go is incredibly hard for people to do; however, learning to let go will be one of the most beneficial things that you will ever do for yourself.

When you let go, you must relinquish the need for control ...

What would your world feel like if you released the need for control over other people, and what they were doing, and you just let go? The responsibility is now off of your shoulders, and you are solely responsible for yourself, and the things that you do. Ah, doesn't it feel nice? Why? Because when you are trying to control a situation or an outcome of a situation that involves other people, you are working with resistance. How do I know this? Because, no one ever has to take "control" of something that is in the state of allowing, when something or someone is in the state of allowing it is flexible and ever changing. When situations, or people, are in a state of allowing they become adaptable. When you are trying to "control" a situation, or a person, or a person's behavior, the amount of energy it takes is exhausting. The worst part is ***control is an illusion;*** you will never be able to control anything, any situation, or anyone without consent. So in actuality there is no control, only consent!

When you let go, you are no longer forcing things to happen (pushing), you relax into a state of allowing (receiving).

When you are trying to force something to happen, you are working against the Universal Laws. Things do not like to be pushed. When pushed, energetically things tend to remove themselves or push back. You cannot push things into your life; the outcome is unfavorable to everyone and everything involved. Why? Because anything being pushed is in a state of resistance and when you are in a state of resistance there will be friction. When you relax into a state of allowing, then you begin to work with the Universal Laws, there is no resistance, and there is no friction, there is only flow. When you allow yourself to *be in the flow of things*, your energy begins to "draw in and attract" instead of "push out and repel." This allows you to draw into your life things that you wish to happen, effortlessly. Allowing things into your life feels fantastic! It feels natural …

When you let go, it allows your energetic river to flow freely.

When you let go, you energetically allow things to flow in and flow out of your life freely. There are no stagnant ponds of energy in your system. This is so beneficial, because it means there is also a consistent flow of new energy streaming into your life. Energy that is fresh and clear, your system needs replenishment for nourishment and for growth. A consistent energetic flow also replaces any old, toxic energy, with new, vibrant energy. It allows your system a way to maintain a clean environment.

When you let go, you welcome change and let your resistance down.

Many people resist change because they know what it is they currently have, and they think, "What if it gets worse?" They never tend to think, "What if it gets a million times better?" So they resist change with all of their might. Change is inevitable and there are so many variables to any situation, things that have never even come across your radar. Since change is inevitable, resisting change does not stop it from happening; it only makes you feel more uncomfortable while it is happening. If you stop resisting change things may not turn out so bad, in fact, you may be pleasantly surprised! Change promotes growth and growth is a good thing. Resistance causes things to break or shatter.

When you let go, you break attachments.

Breaking attachments to something or someone can be incredibly freeing, and energetically you will feel so much lighter! When you are trying with all of your might to hold onto something or someone, you must consistently project a certain amount of energy outward, over and over again, in order to maintain the attachment. This takes a huge amount of effort on your part, especially if the attachment is primarily one sided. You must, in fact, double the amount of energy you would normally send out, because unless the energy is reciprocated, it will die out. In order to maintain this type of attachment, you are either knowingly or unknowingly committed to not letting it die out. Attachments do not promote growth, people use them to try and fill a spiritual void in their life. A spiritual void will never be filled with an attachment; your attention will only be temporarily diverted from it.

When you let go, you allow wasted and toxic energy to die out.

When you focus your attention towards any kind of drama going on in your life (which is extremely common), when you talk about it, discuss it, or give your opinion about it, you are energetically engaging the drama back. When you engage, or reciprocate in any way, it is like throwing fuel on an energetic fire, so to speak. Then, in many instances, you can watch this energetic fire burn out of control and injure innocent people along the way.

"When energy is sent out or focused in your direction, it can only maintain itself for a very brief time, unless (this is important) ... it is somehow engaged upon."

If you are ever around negative people, and they direct a negative comment or action your way, let it go. Do not engage this behavior in any way, shape, or form. These are battles that are never won, they only appear to be won, when someone disengages himself or herself from the battle. Which is exactly what I am suggesting you do, disengage and let it go. Because if you do not disengage, anger, bitterness, and resentment, all of the things that come with engaging in this type of behavior, will then "park" itself in your energetic body. When these types of negative emotions "park" themselves in your body, they will then manifest in your cells, energetic or otherwise. Many times this is where manifestation of illness occurs.

"Energy that is focused upon you or in your direction has to have some energetic reciprocation or it will just die out."

By all means … let it die out!

When to let go …

This is important! When you are focusing your energy towards something that is not manifesting, it is "stuck," or hung up somewhere. You will not be able to control it, force it, resist it, or manifest it into being, it will not happen! People really, really get stuck on this. When you shift your focus away from something that is not manifesting for you at the time, many times it will allow the energy that is "hung up" somewhere to work itself free. If that does not happen, removing your focus will usually allow another avenue to come to light. In either case:

If something is not working after reasonable effort … LET IT GO!

Spiritual Rule #14

Stop Saving Your Happiness For Special Occasions!

"Happiness is a gift from God that has been given to you. You can access it all day, every day if you choose, and live your life in complete and total bliss! Or you can choose to save it and only bring it out for special occasions."

Stop saving your happiness for special occasions!

I am shocked when I see people trying to suppress their laughter. They try and keep some type of composure, or hold their ground, by not laughing! Some people think that being an adult means being responsible, and being serious is acting responsibly, and laughter is not appropriate when you are being serious. Or there are also people who are upset or angry about something and the only way to show how angry or upset they are, is to make sure they repress any signs of joy. Otherwise, they will not make their point effectively! But who is really affected by repressing joy or laughter? The repressor is! So if you ever find yourself holding back a smile or laughter, well, stop doing that! That's just a roundabout way of wanting to control and resist your natural emotions. Who's that good for?

Laughter opens your heart chakra.

Opening your heart chakra is a very important part of working with the Universal Laws and raising your consciousness to a higher level. Chakras are energy centers where your physical body and your etheric body meet. Your etheric body is your "spiritual body." (You can learn more about your chakra system in my book **Keys to the Spirit World**.) When your heart chakra opens, you experience a feeling of happiness flooding over your body and into your soul. It is important for people to learn how to open and close their chakras; you need to exercise them just like you do your muscles. A very simple way to do this is by laughter; laughter opens your heart chakra naturally. If you never open your heart chakra, or suppress opening it by resisting laughter, then your heart chakra becomes harder to open each time. So remember to exercise you heart chakra, not only does it feel good to laugh physically, but it is very important for your heart and your spiritual body.

Laughter raises your vibration.

Everyone vibrates energetically, and laughter raises your vibration. Imagine that you are like a tuning fork, and your vibration can be measured on a scale from one to ten. Let's say that when you vibrate at a level ten, you energetically become a human magnet, powerfully drawing things into your life that you desire. On the other end of the spectrum, when you vibrate at a level one, your magnet has no power; with no power behind your magnet you will have a hard time drawing anything into your life. When you laugh, your magnet hangs out around levels eight to ten, and that could not be more beneficial! When you are offering a higher vibration, things become clearer, the Law of Attraction kicks in, and you naturally tap into your spiritual tools. Laughter is an easy way to raise your vibration.

Enjoy the little joys in life longer.

Sometimes the littlest things can bring you such joy. Those little things should be savored as long as possible, because the more you enjoy the little things, the more they turn into big things! Savor that feeling for as long as you can. It exercises the heart chakra and keeps your vibration high, it helps to keep your mood elevated, and it is good for you on a spiritual and physical level! I get so excited when I receive the artwork for my new book covers, that each time I get a new one I put them up as my screen saver, and on my phone. Then when I answer my phone or open my computer, I have a flood of happiness quickly fill my heart, no matter what mood I am in. Milk the little joys you have in life until you wear them out!

Spiritual Rule #15

Spend Some Time
Creating Your Future!

*"Always keep your focus forward, never in the
past. If you focus on the past it holds you there.
You cannot change the past, that is time wasted.
When you focus forward and spend time creating
your future, that holds value, it is time well spent!"*

Many people ask me, "Where do you think that I should
I be heading in life?"

To which I usually respond, "Well, have you given some
thought to where you would like to be a year from now?"
Then comes the bewildered look, followed by the classic
answer of, "No, guess I never really thought about it."

The reason I start with this question is because I like
to know what their thought process is. This way I can

help them learn what to do, instead of just giving them a quick fix. In my experience people tend to over complicate most things in life, and my rule of thumb is simplify, simplify, simplify! That being said, people need to spend more time clarifying their destination.

How on earth do you expect to get somewhere if you don't know where you are going? Many times people think that they need an expert to tell them what their skills are, or where they should be heading in life. But let's face it, who is the most qualified expert, someone who truly knows what your wants and needs are? You! You are underestimating your own skills! It is not as hard as you think to figure out what fits your current wants and needs; it just takes some time to think it through. More importantly it is FREE! "Excellent!" You are probably thinking, "Now how do I do that?" Well I am going to give you an easy six-step process and here it is.

Six steps to get you headed in the right direction:

1) First of all (again, make sure you do not overcomplicate this), it is a simple process of figuring out what your wants and your needs are. Very simple!

Do you want more time?
Do you need a vacation?

Do you want more stability?

Do you need less stress?

Take some time and figure these things out, and write these things down on a list. Do not rush the process; you might even want to carry a piece of paper around with you for a week, with the idea of completing this task. Because during the day is most likely when you will be able to identify what your wants and needs are. Then jot them down so you don't forget, and go about your day.

2) Spend a few minutes, hours, or weeks and imagine, what would your ideal day be like? Usually this pertains to work, so what would your ideal work day be like?

What kind of hours you would be working?

What time of day would you go to work?

When you would come home?

What type of people would you like to work with?

What type of environment would it be?

Would you be able to use your creativity?

Would it be more structured?

3) Next figure out what your ideal home situation would be.

Would your space be cleaner or more organized?

Would it be larger so that it didn't feel so claustrophobic?
Would you live in the same city, in the same state, or somewhere else?
Would you live with different people?
What feels good to you, or should I say, what feels better to you?

4) Take some time to visualize what it would *feel* like if your ideal day (home and work) was your current reality. *Really let this vision take hold.* Imagine going through a typical workweek, and what you would be doing every day. How does it feel? Ah ... it should feel really nice, because you have created this environment. If it doesn't feel right, start over again, until you get to the "Ah ... that feels good and way less stressful" part! Stay there for a moment, and enjoy the feeling, you should begin to feel your muscles relax and the stress melt away. Then allow yourself to feel the excitement of bringing some new changes into your life, and how good that feels. Breathe in your new life, and exhale the old stress.

5) Every morning or night (I prefer you do both), take a few minutes out of your day and visualize your future, your ideal day/life, a year from now. Spend some time enjoying that feeling everyday. Over time it will begin to feel like your comfortable place, you will enjoy being there. You do not have to do this for a set amount of

time, it can be two minutes or twenty minutes, whatever you desire. A really good time to do this kind of visualizing is during your "falling asleep" time. When you are lying in bed, just about to drift off to sleep, 90 percent of people spend this time going over the stressors of the day and predetermining the stressors of tomorrow. Biggest mistake people make! You are using some of the most valuable time, the alpha brainwave state, to manifest your stressors into your future reality. Let's use it more constructively, shall we?

6) Now that you have some detail and a direction in which way to go, start making choices that align with where you want to see yourself a year from now. Do not self-sabotage out of fear or worry and make choices that do not align with your new destination, out of fear or worry. Most of the time people are in their current situation, whether they want to believe it or not, because of fear and worry. So this is about trying something new and using a different approach. In other words, if you want to live somewhere else, begin to look for other places, or start saving some money, or both. If you want a different job, begin the process of scouting out what fits you better. Tell your friends what it is you are looking for, many times if you follow these steps the Universe will bring opportunity to you, and sometimes that avenue can be through friends or acquaintances.

Make choices that MOVE YOU FORWARD! Because most likely you are currently making choices that are keeping you right where you are, in your current situation.

All of this can be done in your spare time. Many times people do not think they have any spare time, but this is far from the truth. Most people just spend their spare time on Facebook, on the computer, on the phone, or watching TV. I know as well as the next person that when you begin to do any of those things, minutes turn into hours, hours turn into days and days turn into years ... you catch my drift!

Spiritual Rule #16

Get Rid Of Your Poverty Mindset!

"Would you change your thoughts if you knew that they would become a reality? Just something to think about ..."

Are You Cursed With A Poverty Mindset?

Well, first of all let's just disregard the word cursed, because in over forty years of being a psychic I have never seen a curse because they do not exist. (Unless of course you have convinced yourself that they do, then, it is possible in your world, but not in mine. Remember your reality is your perception). However, I did know that it would get your attention. Let's start with the basic issue, is there really a poverty mindset? Absolutely! Now that you know that there is such a thing as a poverty mindset, I am sure many of you are wondering, "Well what is it? Do I have it? I need to get rid of it!"

A poverty mindset is something like this: You are certain that all things related to money are driven by the economy and the economy is bad, so you are doomed to be poor!

For example, do you ever find yourself thinking any of these things?

1) I have always struggled in the past, I am struggling now, and I do not see how it is ever going to change!
2) There are not enough jobs out there, since no one else is getting one, that's a pretty good indicator that I won't get one either.
3) I can never afford anything that I want!
4) Those people (people with money), who live like that are different and have better skills, I never get a break!
5) I want to do XYZ, but I will never be able to because I will never have enough money.
6) I don't see things getting any better for me.
7) The economy is screwed, that means so am I!

It is so important for you to get this, and I really mean GET THIS! Your thoughts do become your reality! Now I am not kidding around here and people need to know this more then ever. *This concept is not metaphysics, this is* *quantum physics and it has been proven on a scientific level!* Secondly, there are more people making more money, every second, of every day, than you can possibly imagine! Now if it is just (physical) law that everyone's finances are dictated by, then this would not be possible! Thirdly, if this is all true, there must be something more out there that dictates our money flow!

Now if you pay close attention to Suze Orman, Rich Dad Poor Dad, Donald Trump, Bill Gates, Warren Buffet, or Sam Walton (I could go on), these people do not think of money in the same manner as 98 percent of the world. They know things, and they try and teach it to people, but for some reason it falls upon deaf ears. This currently does and will always separate the people.

Poverty mindset group (98% of the population):

1) They are sure they are a victim to how money flows to them, the economy, the stock market, gas prices, where they live, etcetera, and they will always be limited as to what flows in to their life. (There is another common poverty mindset word ... limited!)

2) They feel desperate for money; they never have enough, no matter how much they have, they always "need" more.

3) Money becomes a primary focus in their life. (Now that alone can be a huge problem, no matter how rich you are or how poor you are, the more your focus is on cash, I swear ... you will repel it!)

4) Money (or lack of it) is the reason, they believe, they are unhappy! They do not understand that happiness is a choice, not a side effect. There are some people in countries with no running water who are happier than people I know who have clean water anytime of the day or night, they just turn on the faucet and there it is! Amazing!

Now I am not making light of the money thing, you do need money to eat, pay the electricity bill and put a roof over your head. There have been many, many, years that I have lived paycheck to paycheck barely making it, with twenty dollars for the week to spend on groceries. Sometimes you need to work at a job that is low paying or that you do not like in order to make ends meet, but this should be viewed as temporary, not permanent, while you pursue your passion and your dream.

The other 2% of the population:

1) They know and truly believe that money is energy and it is constantly flowing.

2) They believe that there is more than enough to go around, that somehow, it will always work out.

3) They also believe that they are in no way limited to the amount of money that will flow into their life.

4) They do not always need to know how money will flow to into their life, but they know there are many possible avenues, and know somehow it just will.

5) They are not desperate for money, in fact, they are so focused and concentrated on following their passion, or their dream, that money becomes an afterthought, (even while they are sleeping in their car, or on someone else's couch).

6) Passion becomes the focus, even the addiction, and that will most definitely affect your money flow in the opposite direction, a very positive one, given time.

Did you know that many of the richest people in the world were born poor, and they were driven by their passion, (***this is very key here, they were not driven by money, but driven by what they loved doing***). Did you also know that many of them failed, or were so poor while they were on their journey, that they felt they were at rock bottom and the only way to go was up? That their only option was to succeed? Staying at rock bottom was not an option for them. Hmmm ... succeed-ing while poor. Yes, I like that option! Many of these people believe, truly believe, to the bottom of their soul that they are limitless, and that money is not restrictive. They believe their money flow is not tied to the economy or what other people are doing. Poverty mindset people feel very different, they look at money like it is in a clear cube, they know it exists, but it is untouchable. Do you see the difference? They feel to the very core of their soul, that money is untouchable! They know that it is there, they know that the money exists, but they do not feel that they could ever access enough of it in their lifetime, because they cannot *"see"* how it is possible.

Therein lies the difference. People who have acquired large sums of money in their lifetime (some of them started with less then you have right now), never needed to be able to *"see"* how it was possible in order to *"believe"* that it could happen to them. They just *"knew"* that it was, and therefore *"seeing"* it happen became their reality!

Spiritual Rule #17

Love Unconditionally

*"Love has amazing energetic power, thus has
an incredible effect on people. Just remember,
use your powers for good and not evil."*

Have you ever looked up the definition for love? Love is an emotion of strong affection that is based on kindness and compassion. Love is something that refers to a variety of emotions from passion and desire, to intimacy. Love can be a defined as romantic, or platonic, or it can be a strong passionate feeling about a desire or something you are compassionate about. Love can be many of these things and it can also be hard to define on some levels, but one of the ways love is never defined as is "conditional"!

Everyone wants to feel loved. Love is a major component to interpersonal relationships; family relationships, platonic relationships, or intimate relationships, love plays a major role. Love raises your vibration and opens your heart chakra. However, one thing that people do not know is that love is also energy, and as energy it must follow the laws of the Universe. This is important, especially for those wishing to have more love in their life. Energy needs to keep flowing or moving, in fact, it is important. With flow and movement, energy is consistently being replenished. With replenishment, old toxic energy is moved out and new vibrant energy replaces the old. Whatever energy you put out, must be replaced (unless you resist).

Love more.

Love is a very powerful energy! It has an amazing effect on other people, as well as your spiritual and physical body. The more you love the more you activate your heart chakra, which is a very important chakra to exercise. The heart chakra is tied to your higher consciousness, your vibration and your intuition. It also helps to balance all other chakras in your system. The more love you offer, the more you will also receive.

Love unconditionally.

Love as energy takes on a different form when you place conditions on your love. Love cannot be offered with anything other than *love in pure form*. When love is offered with conditions attached, the energy is no longer powerful, it is no longer activating your heart chakra, it becomes something else that you are sending out into the Universe, something else that will also flow back into your life. It becomes toxic love; love that is toxic to your system and others.

Love cannot be held hostage.

Love is not a form of manipulation; love is just that, love. Love in pure form cannot be held hostage. What do I mean by that? Holding love hostage is when you do not like someone else's behavior, so you decide not to "reward" him or her with your love. In other words, if they behave a certain way or do something you don't agree with, you make sure you do not show them any love. That is not love in its pure form; that would be toxic love. You see, love is not trying to manipulate someone else's free will and the choices they make; love is loving someone regardless of their free will choices.

Unconditional love.

When offering love, it is only offered in its purest form when it is offered unconditionally. Will people you love do things you do not agree with? Yes. Will people you love make mistakes? Yes. Will people you love even make bad choices? Yes. That is why we are here on earth as spiritual beings, to potentially do all of those things. Then hopefully we learn and grow, as a result of doing all of those things. To never encounter any disappointment from yourself, or others, is unrealistic. So it is most important for you to love unconditionally, regardless of choice, and regardless of mistakes, because we are all human, and as humans we sometimes make mistakes.

See your loved ones for who they are, not who you want them to be.

It is very important for you to truly *see* your loved ones for who they are, in order to offer pure love unconditionally. Why? Because it helps to eliminate disappointment and expectations on your end. Many times people do not see their loved one for who they are, rather they see them for who they wish them to be. ***Seeing the "potential" in someone does not make your loved one someone other than who they really are***. This implies that they are somehow less than, as a person, or they are somehow a disappointment to you, and others, at the current moment. It also implies there is a possibility, that maybe, someday, if they realize their "potential" they might be this really amazing person! However, for right now, they are just a person with great "potential." This really confuses people. When you see a glimmer of who you think your loved one could be in your mind, that glimmer can take on a whole life of its own and create a whole new being that does not even exist! This often results in disappointment and anger. ***Appreciate your loved ones for who they are not for who you wish them to be.***

Do not mistake manipulation for love.

Pure love cannot be used as a manipulation tactic, toxic love can be. Do not mistake anyone who wishes to change who you are or your behavior in exchange for his or her love, as love in pure form. In fact that is not love at all, it is just manipulation in disguise.

Pure love is offered unconditionally, with no strings attached. There are no guidelines you must follow, or "potential" you must live up to; you are just loved for the simple fact that you exist!

Love more.

Spiritual Rule #17

Spiritual Rule #18

Take Care of Yourself Physically

"It doesn't matter how good of a driver you are if you fail to maintain the vehicle you are driving in. You must maintain spiritual and physical balance in order to perform to the best of your ability. If ignored, you will end up parked along the road somewhere with your hazard lights on."

Balance is key as spiritual beings living in a physical world.

We are spiritual beings, but we do live in a physical world, and this is also important. Your spiritual self is most definitely a huge part of your existence, in fact, it is your existence. However, when living in a physical world there are some other things to consider. One of the things is, your physical body is the vehicle you are given in order to maintain your existence on earth, here in the "physical world." If your vehicle is not properly cared for and maintained, your vehicle will most likely break down at some point in time, potentially affecting the quality of your journey and even the length of your stay.

Many things dictate the way your body operates physically. The spiritual aspect is very important; however, we have covered a lot of that elsewhere in this book. So for the sake of this chapter we are going to cover the physical side here.

Eat right.

When you think of a vehicle or a piece of machinery, you understand that it is important for those things to have oil and gas to allow all of the internal parts of the vehicle to run smoothly. When you look at plants and vegetation, you understand that it is important for the plants to have rich soil full of nutrients, sunlight, and water. Having these things allows the plants to grow and thrive, and with that comes the ability to weather the environment. Your body is no different. You need to make sure that you provide your vehicle, or your body, with food filled with nutrients, and with water. It is important to keep the things that you put into your body as healthy as possible. When you maintain a healthy body, it becomes strong and resilient. This gives your body the ability to weather an environment of toxins or illness rather well. Eating well and making sure you have the right vitamins and minerals should be a part of your physical balance.

Exercise.

Your body is blessed with over six hundred fifty muscles! Your body is a wonderful piece of human machinery. Do you know what happens to machinery when you let it sit for long periods of time without any use? Things become brittle, parts begin to rust, particles accumulate on the surface, and oils dry up. If you allow this to happen with a piece of machinery, when you decide that it is useful again and go to operate the machine, what do you think is going to occur? It is not going to operate well. Again, your body is no different. Your muscles are meant to be used, and in order to use them, they must be maintained. Exercise should also be a part of your physical balance.

A machine is a device consisting of fixed and moving parts that modifies energy and transforms it into a more useful form.

What a wonderful piece of machinery you have, your very own body! Take care of it and appreciate it inside and out. Do not neglect it, and then get frustrated when it is operating at a less than optimal level. Your body is meant to be a useful vehicle that makes your very existence in the physical world possible!

Spiritual Rule #19

Listen To More Music

"When you need a natural mood elevator put on some music. Music makes the soul smile."

Music elevates the soul vibrationally.

Music reaches you on a deeper level then you may even realize. There is a reason music is connected with Angels in the spirit world. Music touches you and elevates you on a soul level. When you are listening to music that you enjoy, it elevates you not from the outside in, but from the inside out! This is a huge benefit to your spiritual and physical being. Because when it resonates with you on a soul level, the chemistry of your body actually changes.

Music is a good distraction from worry.

It is hard to worry and stress out about something when you are listening to music. Your body wants to feel the music, you find yourself wanting to sing the words. You cannot sustain worry and enjoy music at the same time for very long. The stronger one of the two will eventually take over and naturally you will gravitate towards what makes you feel better.

Music affects your emotions, therefore, is a natural mood elevator.

Because of the physical effects music has on your body chemistry it also has an effect on your brain. There have been many studies done on how classical music affects your brain function and emotions. But this actually applies to all music that elevates your soul, or that you personally like. It is a natural mood elevator, without the use of chemicals!

Music research shows it elevates memory, learning, and is good for your cardiovascular system.

There has also been much research done over the years to show how music is good for memory, learning, and your physical body. Music tends to relax the physical body when needed and motivates the brain and the physical body when exercising. Music activates within you personal motivation and strength. They have actually tested this by taking two groups of people exercising, one group

listened to music and the other did not. The group listening to music out performed the group that was not, quite
a bit. Music has been shown to relax the body, showing
changes in heart rate and heart rate variability promoting
cardio health. There have been mountains of research
showing the effects music has on your memory and
learning capacity. I personally have never met anyone
who did not like music of some kind. From the dawn of
man it has been enjoyed. There is proof all over the place
that music is beneficial for you on a spiritual and physical
level, all pointing towards one thing.

Listen to more music!

Spiritual Rule #20

Give and Appreciate

"I love that I can find clean drinking water most everywhere that I go, I love that I do not have to sew, or make my own clothes. I love that I can go into a store and have a million things to choose from to eat without having to grow it, or walk thirty miles for it. We are so blessed!!!"

This chapter is about giving to others and acknowledging what you already have (because let's face it, most days you take for granted that you have a home, running water, and food to eat). Well it is time to wake up and smell the coffee, so to speak!

Today is a day of appreciation. For today, I want you to take the focus off yourself and what you don't have and start looking at other people, and how you might be able to help them. Many people are in the same boat as you are, and many people are in a situation that is much, much, worse! Yes, I said it, much worse! Because if you are reading this book you are not struggling to find clean water to drink; need I say more? This day is not about how you need help, but how you can help one other person, a pay it forward kind of day!

Anyone can do this; you can give money, or time. Here are some ideas:

1) Give money to someone in need. You can give $1, $5, or a $100, it doesn't matter. Not to your kids, or family, this is about giving to someone in need with no ties attached and no need for acknowledgement about the giving. You could tip someone more than usual, or donate some money to charity. However you wish to do it.

2) Give some of your time. If you are a professional, donate fifteen minutes or an hour of expertise. Donate babysitting time or volunteer!

3) Give clothes or items. There are almost always items around your house that you do not use, wear, or need. This is almost always true with toys and clothes. You can give them to a shelter, or to someone moving, toys for tots, Salvation Army, whatever!

4) Give food. Give to someone in need of food, a dinner, or a can of soup. Give whatever you can provide.

A lot of times people feel that a can of soup or a dollar is so little that it does not mean much. This is the wrong perspective; this day is about the intent of helping someone in need, not how much you can give. The intent of helping people is very powerful! Can you imagine if even half of the population did this tomorrow? Can you image the energetic effect that it would have, the love behind the giving and receiving? Powerful!

REMOVE ALL JUDGEMENT!!!! This is not your time to judge why anyone else is in his or her current situation! It is your time to find love in your heart and give from there ... that is all ... nothing less, nothing more. Giving should just be that, giving!

Spiritual Rule #21

Embrace the Power You Hold

"Know there's more, because there is ... Go after what you want, because you can ... Live your dream life, because you're meant to ... Don't settle, because everyone else does."

You are not a victim of life! So don't act like it!

The strong and the weak are not made somehow genetically different or spiritually different from one another. The difference between the strong and the weak is that *the strong utilize the power they have, and the weak deny they have any power at all!* You were born with gifts and abilities, use them. You were created with spiritual tools, use them. What you don't know, learn, and what you learn, teach!

Embrace the power you hold!

You have the power to become who you want to be.

You have the power to be successful.

You have the power to thrive.

You have the power to keep going.

You have the power to resist.

You have the power to stop.

You have the power to fail.

You have the power to give up.

You are blessed with power. It's up
to you how it will be used.

You are powerful beyond belief!

Appendix 1

21 Commandments To Your Happiness!

1) I understand I am a reflection of my choices.

2) I will not let my relationship status define my happiness.

3) I have removed all contingency clauses previously attached to my happiness.

4) I release myself from all expectations.

5) I will not hold anyone else responsible for my happiness.

6) I will always be pursuing at least one of my dreams.

7) I will experience happiness in the present.

8) I will protect myself from other people's negative thinking.

9) I will not take other people's unhappiness personally.

10) I will implement change.

11) I will not let fear bully me.

12) I will worry less.

13) I will let things go.

14) I will stop saving my happiness for special occasions.

15) I will spend time creating my future.

16) I will rid myself of a poverty mindset.

17) I will love unconditionally.

18) I will take care of myself physically.

19) I will listen to more music.

20) I will give and appreciate.

21) I will embrace the power I hold!

Appendix 2

Do You Feel Like You Are In a Rut?

What in the world is happening? I am encountering many, many people who are experiencing the same thing around the world. It is a flurry of undirected energy! I have friends and colleagues who are wondering, what's this all about? I am normally focused, I can usually get things done in a timely manner, but lately I feel like I am going in circles!

This can happen when you are feeling a flurry of undirected energy and it can result in people feeling like they are in a rut. I have received quite a few emails asking for me to elaborate a bit more on some steps to take when you feel this way. So here are some easy steps that you can take, broken into two different categories. Why two categories, you may wonder? The first one will be for linear thinkers; these people like to think things through on a more practical level instead of spiritual. The second category is for the more spiritually based thinkers. Now keep in mind that it is most effective if you just do all of these things, or at least some of the things from each category.

Linear Based Thinkers:

1) Educate yourself more on the relationship between energy and money. Money is energy! Most well-known financial advisors like Suze Orman and Rich Dad Poor Dad talk about money as an energy. This is why money is also referred to as currency.

2) Shift your perspective and take your power back. You are not a victim unless you allow yourself to be!

3) Get rid of the mind clutter! What is most important to you at this time of your life? Do you need to get bills paid, more freedom, more time, etcetera. Then create a list and prioritize the list from top to bottom, most important things first. Focus on tackling the things at the top of your list, then working your way through to the bottom. Many people just feel like they have a barrel full of issues to deal with and no organization, so they have no idea where to start. When you have no organization this leads to something that I like to call "mind clutter." The problem with mind clutter is that it will leave you feeling really overwhelmed,

and with no clear starting point, it's just easier to put things off over and over again. Then your barrel gets really full and that can lead to major stress or anxiety.

4) Prioritize yourself and implement the 75/25 rule. What is the 75/25 rule? You commit 75 percent of your free time focusing on yourself and 25 percent of your free time helping others. Why? Because most people commit more free time to helping others than they commit to making their own life better. When you fly on an airplane, during the safety instructions the stewardess will say, "Make sure to put your own oxygen mask on first before you help others, in case of emergency." It is similar to this, you cannot help other people when your own life is in shambles, or you are unhappy. Why? Because, even though you might beg to differ, it is not effective, period! It is way more effective to help others when you have it together. Let's face it, how well would you take relationship advice from your cousin who is an unhappy, self-proclaimed, serial dater? That advice is not nearly as effective as the advice coming from Grandma and Grandpa who have been married for forty-five years! Especially when it seems that they have truly experienced the ups and the downs of a relationship and how to deal with them in a successful manner. If you are the cousin, then let's get it together!

Energetic Development (Spiritually Based Thinkers):

1) Break Inertia! What does that mean? Do something different, switch up your daily routine. If you are sluggish, get moving, if you are hyperactive, be still. For instance, if you normally exercise at night, then start doing it in the morning for a while. If you don't exercise at all, then take a walk, jog, ride a bike, or play tennis twice this week. If you normally do house work in the evening, do it in the morning. Break boring repetitive patterns and choose a challenge. *Power is seldom developed by clinging to security,* give up being safe, and your power chakra (your third chakra) will awaken more quickly!

2) Avoid invalidation and criticism from those who do not understand your situation, especially if you are a sensitive person who takes things to heart. When you are undertaking something new and uncertain, invalidation and criticism can be an instant power crippler!

3) Make sure your energy travels in a complete circuit! In other words, what you put out comes back; remember the 75/25 rule.

4) Both effort and resistance are tiring and wear your energy down. That is a sign that your power is not flowing harmoniously. *When you find yourself strain-*

ing with effort, stop! Think about what you are doing and imagine doing it without effort – smoothly and enjoyably. (Morning meditation.)

5) Morning meditation! This is really important, and believe me, I have gotten busy myself and skipped it. Boy is that an instant reminder of why not to skip morning meditation; I think it's as bad as skipping breakfast! Take a minute, two minutes, or five minutes, whatever you want, and sit quietly in a chair. When you do this I want you to imagine your day going exactly the way that you want it to. (See Appendix 3.)

6) Attention … attention focuses energy! Pay it when it needs to be paid and give it to yourself. Notice where it goes, the rest of the energy will surely follow.

7) Grounding brings us into the present. Of course there is meditation for grounding, but you can also go jogging, power walking, or do ab workouts.

You will probably not do all of these things overnight, but pick the ones that resonate with you and start doing those things right away. You will surely begin to notice a difference!

Appendix 3

What Is Meditation?

Meditation is a practice of sitting quietly while regulating your breath using intone mantras or visualization in attempts to harmonize your mind, body, and soul.

Why is this important? Because meditation is really effective in clearing out mind clutter as well as energetic clutter. It is knocking out two birds with one stone so to speak, on a spiritual and physical level. You clean your house, take showers, eat right, and maintain your physical health by getting the proper rest, etcetera. Well, equally important to your physical and spiritual health, is to keep your mind and your energetic field as clutter free as possible. This will allow you to operate at your most efficient level.

Meditation synchronizes brain wave patterns.

There have been extensive studies done on meditation over many, many years, and the most interesting findings seem to show in the EEG measuring of brain wave patterns. During your waking consciousness, brain waves are random and chaotic. The brain usually operates with different wavelengths from the front to the back of the brain, and from hemisphere to hemisphere. Meditation changes this drastically. Subjects in meditation show increased alpha waves, and these waves continue to increase throughout the duration of the meditation. Also, the front and the back of the brain begin to synchronize as well as the left and the right hemispheres. In other words, the different areas of your brain begin to work together synchronistically! After a few months, this integration in the brain is not just noticed during the meditation state but during daily activity as well.

Meditation has spiritual and physical health benefits.

Meditation has also been linked to lowering blood pressure and helping with anxiety and depression, just to name a few. Not to mention the spiritual aspects of raising your vibration, intuitive development, and raising your consciousness.

Meditation Exercise

I have designed a meditation exercise to help you work more efficiently with the Universal Laws. I suggest doing some type of meditation at least once a day. I personally recommend meditating in the morning if you only have time for one meditation. Morning meditation, I have noticed, definitely sets the tone of your day.

Before you begin, find a quiet place where you will not be disturbed. You will be using a chair for this meditation, so find a comfortable chair to sit in, then place both feet flat on the floor.

1) Define what it is that you want to achieve in your meditation. This is a very important step whether it is calmness, joy, better health, or happiness; whatever it is that you desire. It is very important because intent is what actually creates anything whether it is in the spiritual or physical realm.

2) Sit comfortably in a chair or in an upright position in a quite place.

3) Close your eyes and concentrate on your breathing. Slow your breathing to a relaxed state.

4) Once your breathing is rhythmic, concentrate on relaxing all of the muscles in your body.

5) Imagine that your spine is like a string on a musical instrument. Imagine that this string or cord attaches all of your chakras together, from your root chakra to your crown chakra.

6) Visualize this string or cord vibrating. Imagine that you are in control of how fast or slow the vibration is. Next raise this vibration to the highest level of vibration that you can achieve.

7) When you are vibrating at a high level, imagine that you can see a river above your body. Imagine that this river is the river of the Universe. This river of the Universe contains all of the Universal energy.

8) Then visualize that you are attaching your energy to the Universal River. When you attach your energy with the Universal River, feel yourself flowing in harmony with the Universal Laws.

9) From that state imagine whatever it is that you desire being attracted to you. Imagine that your desires are coming to you as if you are a human magnet.

10) Remain in this state until you feel a sense of completion, then release this image into the Universe.

You should not set a time limit on how long or short your meditation should be, just do what feels right. For many people it will change each day, some days it might be twenty minutes while others it might be two minutes.

Inspirational Quotes

by
Jennifer
O'Neill

Achieve Believe Inspire

How To Use
This Section
of the Book:

This book holds wonderful messages for you from Spirit. You may enjoy this book in two different ways:

1) You may read it from beginning to end like you do with most books, and you will find many messages that will pertain to your everyday life.

2) You can see what messages this book holds for you daily, weekly or just when needed. This book was written with the intention of helping you to receive messages from Spirit when you most need them. When in need, run your finger along the pages of the book until you feel the urge to stop, then open the book and look at the page to see what message is waiting for you ... Thank Spirit for the message, and close the book until it is needed again.

Suggested use for this book is weekly. For instance, beginning of week for inspiration going into the week, or end of the week for inspiration to help you shift your perspective on things encountered throughout the week, or both!

Now see what messages Spirit holds for you ...

"Never worry that your dreams are too big. The Universe and Spirit do not understand limitations…PEOPLE invented limitations!"

"You would not want to be responsible for someone else's happiness, so please do not hold someone else responsible for yours!"

"One of the biggest favors that you can do for yourself is to accept your loved ones for who they are, and not be constantly disappointed because they are not who you think they should be."

"Judgment gives you a very good insight on what a person is really about. Not of the person being judged, but of the person doing the judging."

"Unhappiness can be like a virus spreading from one person, to the next person, to the next one, and so on. When someone is mean or rude to you, do not let their unhappiness infect your own life. If you are the unhappy one, please quarantine yourself so you do not infect others!"

"Love has amazing energetic power, thus has an incredible affect on people. Just remember, use your powers for good and not evil."

"Would you change your thoughts if you knew that they would become a reality? Just something to think about..."

"Why is it that people think staying in a bad relationship is better than being single? Don't they know that being single is the first step to finding a great relationship?"

"When you follow your dream, life is easy. When you follow someone else's dream, life is unsatisfying. When you forget to dream, life is just plain confusing!"

"Sometimes signs from the Universe can be so clear that it seems unrealistic, so we brush them off and call it a coincidence. When really we should change the definition of coincidence to say: Signs from the Universe!"

"Being in a relationship is like getting a new car. In the beginning you are proud of it, you tend to it, and you appreciate and admire it. Later, after the newness wears off you begin to take it for granted, you no longer tend to it and it looses its luster. But remember, your old car is always new to someone else…"

"When you are at the mercy of the Universe and timing, sometimes it feels like the Universe's watch is not working properly because things are not happening fast enough. Did you ever stop to think that maybe your internal clock is not working, because you set it ten minutes ahead of the Universe?"

"Happiness is a gift from God that has been given to you. You can access it all day, every day if you choose, and live your life in complete and total bliss! Or you can choose to save it and only bring it out for special occasions."

"Sometimes the littlest things can bring you such joy! Those little things should be savored as long as possible, because the more you enjoy the little things, the more they turn into big things!"

"Life is much more challenging and complicated in your head, then it is in actuality."

"Letting go is a lot harder than holding on..."

"If you tend to be running into a lot of road blocks lately try a different path, don't just give up. The Universe will sometimes put a roadblock in your path in order to get you to take a different route, not necessarily to get you to change your destination."

"It can be so frustrating if you are not where your want to be in life. Hang in there, because timing is everything. Just keep moving forward, goal in mind, and things will eventually fall into place."

"When you are having a difficult time making a decision, try following your heart center instead of forcing your mind to think through it. You will know it is a good decision if it feels right in your heart Sometimes your head has ulterior motives!"

"Never compare your life to someone else's life. Your journey is unique and one of a kind, no two people will have the same one. That's what makes your life special!"

"People spend an amazing amount of time worrying, waiting, feeling hopeless, and being involved in family or friend drama, without even realizing it. If they spent that same amount of time and energy enjoying life, or thinking about and creating their future, success would be inevitable!"

"Love is allowing mistakes to be made, and allowing growth to happen as a result of mistakes being made..."

"Going against what someone wants you to do is not always disrespect, sometimes it is just self preservation."

"When you are relaxed about where you are in life, things tend to flow more fluidly. It is like if you poke three holes in a bucket of water, the same amount of water is going to flow out the holes whether you just let it flow or you shake the bucket. The difference is the amount of turmoil on the inside of the bucket!"

"Different people have different effects on us since we are all energetic beings. Look at it this way; imagine people's energy as if they are rays from the sun. You can put on a hat and sunscreen, then go out and enjoy the day. Or you can just go right out, get burned, and be miserable for the rest of the week. You don't need to stay indoors, you just need to limit your exposure to the harmful rays!"

"When you are focusing on something in your life, your thoughts send out energy waves. These energy waves are creating life as you know it. The Universe cannot tell the difference between if you want something to happen, or you do not want something to happen, it just responds. Want to know what you've been focusing on? Look around your life."

"You only have one plate to fill, if you fill it with everyone else's stuff, there will not be enough room for you own stuff."

"Why does everyone hate change? It makes us uncomfortable and afraid. When things change, we are forced to adapt and make adjustments in our life. Your perception of change is what brings about fear. So is change the problem or your perception of change?"

"Each and every one of us is born with a unique gift that nobody else has. You are unique because you are the only one with that particular gift. It is our job to figure out what that gift is and develop it. This is what makes our soul in harmony with the Universe."

"Just remember whether it is a good thing or a bad thing, you are who you think you are."

"If you are having a really hard time in your relationship or with your job, is it because you need to change your attitude? Or is it just time to move on? A lot of times people overlook the obvious because the fear of the unknown is terrifying!"

"Where do you see yourself in five years if you continue going down the same road you are currently on? Are you happy with what you see? If not, now is a good time to jump in the drivers seat and take a different route!"

"Try your best not to take other people's unhappiness personally..."

"If you are confused about what you want to do in life, and undecided on what path to take, don't be surprised when if feels like you are going in circles. The Universe is a mind reader!"

"You simply will not be able to please everybody all of the time. It is not the Universe's desire that you do so, it's your desire."

"Imagine the Universe is a river—when you want something so badly, it is like trying to force the river to flow in a certain way. What you need to do is let it go, take a ride on the river and see where it takes you. You can choose the boat in which you ride; you can choose when to jump aboard, but you cannot change the flow of the river, it is too powerful!"

"Some people mesh well together in relationships, friendships, or families and some people do not. People are like ingredients, when mixed together they can either compliment each other, and make something amazing, or create something that just leaves a bad taste in your mouth."

"Every single day of your life you can find one or more reasons to be unhappy. Happiness is not bought, given, earned or learned—it is a state of mind based on your perspective. Happiness is simply a choice..."

"When hungry, if you just wait for fish to jump in your boat, you are going to starve to death. However, if you throw in your fishing line and imagine what a wonderful dinner you are going to have, the Universe will send many fish your way!"

"Action is a key component to the Law of Attraction. Trying to make the Law of Attraction work for you, without taking any action towards your goal, is like having a car with an empty gas tank. It may start up on fumes, but it is not going to take you where you want to go."

"You are the CEO of your life, the head of the company. The pros are: You are in charge, so you can create your life any way that you choose, and reap the rewards if it is going well. The cons are: You are in charge, so if things are going badly, you can blame everyone else all you want, but ultimately you are responsible!"

How To Use This Section of the Book:

"When you are anxious about something, your mind lacks focus, when your mind lacks focus, the Universe receives no direction. Channel your anxiety into creating the outcome that you desire. This will create focus, and focus creates direction."

"You encounter problems everyday, from little ones to big ones. Where do the problems stem from? Your perception. What you think are problems, are really just things that need to be resolved, handled, or tended to, and that's just life! You're not a problem solver; you are a life manager, and managing your life is a wonderful job to have!"

"Do you see the people in your life for who they really are, or do you see them how you want them to be? Never keep someone in your life because you are expecting them to change, keep them in your life because you appreciate them regardless of change!"

"99% of the drama in your life is not caused by someone else. It is caused by your reaction to something, or someone else. Will it matter a year from now? What will matter a year from now will be that you shifted your focus away from your own destination. What is more important, your destination or the drama?"

"Never mind other people's beliefs and opinions, it is really none of your concern. Just because people are not in agreement with you, does not always make you right and them wrong, or them right and you wrong. It just makes you different and diversity is a good thing."

"Imagine your future is like a big lump of clay on a potter's wheel, and you are the potter. God already knows your desire, and has given you the skill and the tools to create that desire. You can put your trust in God and give the potter's wheel a whirl, or you can stare at the wheel, and convince yourself that you are not a potter!"

"Sometimes people spend so much time being miserable about where they are at in their life, that they forget to enjoy the best part. It's kind of like if you are on a road trip and you are so focused on getting to your destination, that you forget to enjoy the reason you are on the road trip in the first place, the journey itself!"

"When you need a natural mood elevator put on some music. Music makes the soul smile."

"We are all students of the Universe, continuously learning and gaining knowledge. Strive to be the best student that you can be. You cannot be a good student if you already know everything."

"Never let being rejected by anyone devalue who you are, whether it be by family, friends or strangers. Someone else's perception of you does not define who you are, or what you can become. God has created each and every one of us with our own unique talents and abilities, and that is something to be valued!"

"Not everybody has to like you, and if someone doesn't like you, it doesn't matter. Billions of people are connecting with each other every day and the good thing is, we are not all the same! However, if you want everyone to like you, the bad thing is, we are not all the same. What does matter is that you like yourself!"

"How much resentment or anger do you have from something that has happened in the past? If you hold on to these feelings, it brings the past into the present. If it is in the present, it will become your future. Don't let your emotional ties to the past keep you from moving forward. You cannot change the past, but the past can change your future, so it's time to leave the past where it belongs, in the past."

"How many little things or tasks do you need to finish? A little thing will stay in the back of your mind as an irritation until it is finished, and this affects you energetically. Imagine that each irritation is like carrying a rock in your pocket, and with each rock you are being weighed down. Take the time to free yourself of the rocks, you will feel so much lighter!"

"When you feel yourself beginning to get upset by your job, a relationship, or life, it usually means change is inevitable. You need to stop and think, what needs to be different in order to help me feel better? Be specific! Don't focus on how it needs to happen, but on the outcome itself. Emotions can be used to fuel a problem or to eliminate it."

How To Use This Section of the Book:

"Life is like a blank sheet of paper. You can view it like art, put it on an easel and create something amazing—or you can just carry it around with you as scratch paper and let people scribble whatever they want to on it."

"Belief—Work hard to create abundance and happiness will follow. (This usually results in disappointment and frustration!) Universal Law—Enjoy life, find happiness and abundance will follow. (Sounds too easy, but you have nothing to lose!) Conclusion—Good time to challenge your beliefs!"

"When your body is feeling extremely tired, or you are very stressed, this means your energy is depleted. It is the Universe's way of telling you to relax, slow down for a minute and recharge. It is like when the gaslight comes on in your car. If you do not take the time to stop and refuel, your car will eventually refuse to take you anywhere!"

"Always keep your focus forward, never in the past. If you focus on the past it holds you there. You cannot change the past, that is time wasted. When you focus forward and spend time creating your future, that holds value, it is time well spent!"

"Fear is driven by people who do not truly understand the Laws of the Universe. Because if they did, they would understand that you get what you focus upon, whether it be fear or abundance...there is plenty to go around!"

"Many people follow each other's beliefs because they feel lost. What they don't realize is, a lot of the time the people they are following are going in circles."

"Why is it that you hold onto things that are not good for you, like a job or a relationship? It's because you already know what you have. If you let go you do not know what you are going to get. Why assume that if you make a change it could be worse. What if it is a million times better?"

"When looking for a job, if you search for something based on your passion and what you enjoy, money will be sure to follow. If your search is based on money or desperation, stress will be sure to follow."

"Why is it that most people spend more time trying to decide what they want for lunch, then they do deciding what qualities they would like in a potential partner. With lunch people are very picky, they know what they like and what they don't like. When it comes to dating they are like—Whatever! They look cute! Then they complain when the Universe sends them, whatever!"

"When you allow the little things in life to fill your heart with joy, it holds an amazing power. Your heart center takes on the vibration of happiness, and when this happens, it will super charge The Law of Attraction. Any desires that you have are sent out into the Universe with a different intensity, the key is to maintain this momentum. Constant Happiness = Consistent Momentum."

"When you get a lot of advice from friends/family, it sways your perspective and it can take you away form your own internal guidance system. If you were driving your car and got lost would you turn on your perfectly working GPS system and follow it? Or would you leave it off, call your friend and ask, what does your GPS system say I should do?"

"Sometimes the Universe takes you in a direction that you are not sure you want to go. This is what happens when you cannot see the destination. Sometimes it's best to stop worrying, and trust the Universe. It has roads to get you from one destination to another, that you never even knew existed!"

"When you get caught up in trying to make everyone else happy, your kids, spouse, family, boss, etc., you forget what makes you happy. Happiness is your foundation. Its like when you build a house, it does not matter how big and beautiful the outside of the house is, if the foundation is weak and the house is in constant need of repair."

"Sometimes friends or family can be like weeds in a garden. Weeds compete for nutrients, water, sun and space. They rob the soil so much, that it makes it hard for the healthy plants to grow. Remove anything from your garden that affects your ability to thrive and grow. Let them fight and compete in someone else's garden."

"When you are working with the Universal Laws, it feels like when you go see a funny movie. You laugh, you enjoy the journey, and the ending always seems to work out. When you are working with the Physical Laws, it feels like when you go see a scary movie. You spend most of your time being afraid, and bracing for the worst possible outcome."

"The key to letting your resistance down is to trust. The key to trust, is allowing yourself to believe in a higher power. The key to believing in a higher power, is knowing that all that you see is not man-made!"

"When working with the Universal Laws you are working with the laws of manifestation, not instant gratification..."

"You can spend a huge amount of time, and energy, convincing yourself and other people why you CANNOT do, or accomplish something. Just once, spend that same amount of time and energy convincing yourself how you CAN do, or accomplish that very same thing and see what happens!"

"Life can be filled with abundance, or not enough. Life can be limitless, or have limits. Life can be happy, or unhappy. It has nothing to do with what you can and cannot see, life is what you perceive it to be."

"You are given a manual (intuition) to help guide you. But, instead of using it, people go about life the hard way. It's like buying something unassembled, and promptly throwing out the instructions (because that is what everyone else did), then getting frustrated, because you are having trouble putting it together."

"Why is it so hard for people to believe life should be easy, and so easy for people to believe life should be hard?"

"You have the power to become who you want to be, you have the power to be successful, you have the power to thrive, you have the power to keep going, you have the power to resist, you have the power to stop, you have the power to fail, you have the power to give up. You are blessed with power, it's up to you on how it will be used."

"Believing you are limited makes the world go round. Believing anything is possible makes the Universe go round."

"Thinking is contagious, so choose whom you surround your-self with carefully! Or at least take precautions, so as not to infect yourself with other peoples' thinking!"

"Some of the best things in life are free; friends, family, pets, the sun, the moon, laughing, smiling, making someone smile or laugh, kissing, loving, singing, hiking, the beach, nature, hearing and seeing all of these things. Enjoy your day!"

"When you are unsure about what you want in life, how do you expect to attract it?"

"When s@#* happens, it is easy to panic. Panic creates fear, and fear is then projected into the future. At this very moment you are creating your future. Do not see your future through the eyes of fear, see your future through the eyes of a creator. The future is created through the eyes of the beholder!"

"It doesn't matter how fast you get somewhere, if you end up at the wrong destination."

"You are the creator of your life! Life does not just happen to you, it is created by you! Imagine that your life is like a book, and you need to fill in all of the chapters. People spend so much time trying to fill in the chapters for everyone else's book, that they leave their own blank! Then they get upset when their life story did not turn out the way they wanted it to, because it was filled in by everybody else."

"Negative thoughts breed negative thoughts, and positive thoughts breed positive thoughts. When you are aware of this, you will become aware of the ultimate power that you hold over your own life!"

"One of the biggest obstacles you will face in life is fear. Fear is an "emotion" based on your "perception" of potential danger. Perception is your own internal view of the world. Talk about battling with your inner self!"

"How you feel about yourself will have a direct affect on your day, your relationships, and your perspective. It is very important to how your life flows, yet it seems to be very unimportant as far as where it lies on people's priority list. Do not underestimate the power of feeling good about yourself..."

"When in limbo, let the Universe decide..."

"Do not try and micro manage the little details in your life. It's not worth the anxiety and frustration that it causes."

"Making someone feel guilty is just a fancy form of manipulation. You make them feel bad AND get them to take responsibility for it! Next time someone tries to make you feel guilty about something, consider the source, then consider the intent behind the source, you will usually find it is not worth your time."

"Life is not so hard. When you stop pushing against it."

"If you do not hold yourself in the highest regard, do not expect anyone else to."

"In order to work successfully with the Laws of the Universe you must relinquish your need for control, it is non-negotiable."

"When working with the Universal Laws, your life mission is the pursuit of happiness. When working with the Physical Laws, your life mission is the pursuit of relationships, marriage, money, house, car, job, making spouse happy, making family happy, status, boat, etc, etc, etc..."

"When you live in a world guided by Physical Laws, other people's opinions can hold the weight of gold to you. When you live in a world guided by the Universal Laws, other people's opinions do not hold much weight at all, they are irrelevant to who you are and where you are going."

"Imagine that your life is like a road trip, with a specific destination in mind. Each time you allow people in your life to give you their opinion on what you're doing, or where you are going, it adds fog. The more opinions, the heavier the fog. The next thing you know, you can't even see the road signs anymore."

"Just because you cannot see the light at the end of the tunnel, does not mean that it is not there. Maybe your tunnel has a lot of curves in it and the light is right around the corner!"

"Everyone experiences failure and disappointment in their life. What is it that separates the people that achieve success, and the people who do not? Two things. 1) They have unconditional faith when others need a reason to believe. 2) They are persistent."

"Frustration is usually a result of your own impatience!"

"When people decide to find peace within themselves, then, you will begin to find peace around the world..."

"Finally, see the light at the end of the tunnel, find your way out... another tunnel...this time grab a flashlight (makes things easier)... start over again! You can never avoid more tunnels, the key is to get smarter with each one!"

"No one wants to jump into a river of negativity, that is why it is usually camouflaged as positive until you make the leap, then the current is strong! But do not be fooled into thinking you are weaker than the current, for you are equipped with the ability to stand up and walk out of the river. It is called free will, and it will trump negativity any day!"

"Sometimes life's most amazing opportunities can scare the daylights out of you, so if you are afraid, it may be time to move out of your comfort zone."

"Isn't it interesting how other people's problems become your problems, when they really had nothing to do with you in the first place."

"When offering help to someone, do it with no strings attached. Because what you fail to realize is that these strings, whether they are big or small, are usually directly linked to your heart or ego, and the slightest tug will cause you discomfort."

"Many times people do not want for themselves what you want for them. For that reason, it is important to be at peace with other people's choices, even if you do not agree with them or understand them."

"Your job in life is to find happiness. Do not mistake this as being a part time job, it is a full time job. The hard part is knowing this and watching other people not take their job seriously. You know, showing up late, leaving early, then always complaining about how unhappy they are!"

"Trying to guide yourself through life using just your mind, makes things hard, because your mind tends to be cluttered with beliefs and opinions. Imagine muddy water flowing through a riverbed filled with piles of sticks and debris, the flow is obstructed. Now imagine running clear water through the same riverbed, it flows with ease. Your intuition is always clear. Which water makes the most sense to run through your riverbed?"

"Everyone encounters stress during their lifetime, some people just hide it really well. So it's not a matter of who has stress in their life, it's a matter of how you handle the stress that you do have. You can allow stress to define who you are. Or, you can view stress as an indicator that you need to make a few adjustments."

"Listening and hearing are very different things, so just because somebody listens to you, do not assume that they heard what you said."

"You would be concerned if your child was consistently angry, cranky, or negative about their life. You know this would have an effect on their health, happiness and ability to cope. As adults, people are like this on a daily basis, and yet it doesn't seem to concern anybody. They think it's normal!"

"True happiness has no conditions attached."

"In a new relationship the major focus is on all the wonderful qualities that your significant other has, so much so, that it overlooks anything negative. When the newness wears off the major focus is on all the negative qualities that your significant other has, so much so, that it overlooks anything positive."

"Isn't it ironic how doing what's best for someone else can be so hard on you."

"When your identity is your own, created based on who you are, there is not a better feeling in the world. When your identity is borrowed, based on who someone else is, or who you wished you were, the opposite rings true."

"The things that you pay the most attention to in your life are the things that manifest and become your reality. Yet the things that you DON'T want to happen in life, are the things you pay the most attention to."

"It is very common for people to overestimate the influence they have on other peoples' happiness, and underestimate the influence that they have on their own happiness."

"The Universe works in mysterious ways! Don't question it, just go with the flow and see where it takes you!!! Sometimes the fun is not knowing where it's going to take you. If you worry too much, you take all the fun out of it!"

"Since the Universe is much larger then the Earth, and it makes the very existence of the Earth possible, doesn't it make sense that the Universal Laws probably have a great impact on our Physical Laws, and what is possible? Think Bigger!!"

"Joy is doing something that you are passionate about, not just pleasing other people. If you please other people in the meantime, well, that's just a bonus!"

"Why is it that people care so much what other people think of them? Especially, since the people who feel the need to make it known what they think about you in the first place, are usually people that are not exactly in a position to be throwing stones..."

"Settling is not what life is about. Settling is what you do when you think that getting what you want out of life, just sounds too good to be true."

"Enjoy the moment. Everyone has become so busy looking ahead and worrying about their future, and looking at yesterday to see what went wrong, that they are forgetting to enjoy today."

"You are a reflection of your choices..."

"Everyone holds the same amount of power and influence over their own lives, it's your perception that differs."

"People usually know what they want, it is the thought of displeasing others that usually stops them from going after it. That's when it is time to decide, is it more important to be happy, or to live your life trying to please others? Because many times you cannot do both."

"Sometimes when you are putting things off, the Universe likes to give you a little shove, that's when it's saying to you, the timing is good now!"

"Worry is something that you should just not make time for. Emotions are food for the Soul. Think of it this way, every time that you worry, you are feeding your Soul empty calories. Then you run around wondering why you feel so crappy all of the time."

"Getting caught up in life, and experiencing life, are two very different things. When you are caught up in life, you are wrapped up in a whirlwind of what everyone else is doing. When you are experiencing life, you are having so much fun, it doesn't matter what everyone else is doing."

"Be selective when sharing your dream with friends and family. You never want to allow anyone the opportunity to make you doubt yourself!"

"Happiness is a choice, not a side effect..."

"Working with the Universe is kind of like when you take a trip on an airplane. You must trust your pilot and have faith that they will get you to your destination, through clouds, rain, snow, turbulence, etc. Imagine you are taking a trip on the Universe's airline; you can watch a movie, sit back and enjoy the ride. Or pace the isles, worrying and panicking that you are never going to get where you want to go."

"Excuses are for people who refuse to take responsibility for the choices that they have made. When you choose wisely, an excuse is not needed."

"Fortunately, I have my positive shield up today. Your negativity will not be able to penetrate it!"

"When the energy around you is a whirlwind of chaos, it is important to keep your focus. Imagine walking in a snowstorm from one building to another. Focus on the door, don't panic, move forward, and do your best to ignore the elements around you. When you allow yourself to get caught up in the elements, it is easy to lose your focus, becoming lost and disoriented."

"Do you ever feel like you are sitting in a fishing boat that has a hole in the bottom, and is filling with water. You are bailing water with a bucket as fast as you can, when you realize, you are the one who created the hole in the first place. The good thing is, since you made the hole, you also have the power to put a plug in it."

"It's not about if you have chaos in your life, it's about how well you manage it."

"You can find value in any experience that you have, you just have to look."

"When you have no knowledge of the Universal Laws, your thinking will mirror your environment, leaving you to feel powerless. Your environment will mirror your thinking, when you understand the Universal Laws, because it is there, that you discover how truly powerful you really are."

"Blaming is so much easier then taking responsibility, because if you take responsibility, then you might be to blame."

"Your life is like a your own reality show, you are the writer, producer, and casting director. You can create your own comedy, or your own drama. Since you are obviously a part of other peoples lives, it might be wise to steer clear of those who enjoy the Soap Opera category, because those themes tend to take a lot of energy, go on forever, and waste many precious hours that you cannot get back!"

"A comfort zone is your own personalized way of setting limitations for yourself!"

"Finding happiness is not for everyone. For some people accepting unhappiness is just much easier."

"All of the hurdles in your mind that you need to overcome, you've put there."

"It's interesting how many times people force their expectations on other people. Then proceed to get mad, because the other people did not live up to their expectations."

"Stress is usually just a negative assumption of what is 'potentially' in your future. Unless you think about it long enough. Then Universal Law dictates that it 'becomes' your future."

"Don't over-think it..."

"Today many people will spend their time trying to handle their future, instead of handling what is front of them at that moment. Tomorrow, those same people will stress out about the things that were left unfinished from yesterday."

"They say life is like a big party! That would explain why many people behave like they are hung over, tired, cranky, and not feeling too good!"

"Nourishment of the Soul is incredibly important to thriving in your environment. You and you alone are responsible for your own Soul nourishment, this is a job that cannot be given to someone else."

"Many times people are trying to fix people who do not wish to be fixed. Those people are usually quite content where they are at, you are just uncomfortable watching them stay there."

"What's worse than bad planning? Making no plan at all, for fear of bad planning."

"Everybody makes a difference in the world throughout their lifetime. The question should not be "if" you are making a difference in this world. The question should be, are you happy with the difference you are making?"

"As children your biggest concern is how much fun you are having, and you care very little about how much you have. As an adult your biggest concern is how much you have, and you care very little about how much fun you are having."

"When you are trying to force yourself down life's path too fast, you will usually miss a corner and derail awhile. The only way to get back on track, is to let your resistance down, and go with the natural flow of the Universe...then...you will gain some momentum!"

"Never compare your life to someone else's life based on what you think you see. Because what you see when you look at someone else's life, is an illusion, based on your perception. More often than not, it's just that. Your illusion, not their reality."

"Steer clear of people sulking in their own misery, unless you wish it to become yours."

"Assuming that you are on the same page as someone else, does not mean that you are. Many times you're not even in the same chapter!"

"I love that I can find clean drinking water most everywhere that I go, I love that I do not have to sew, or make my own clothes. I love that I can go into a store and have a million things to choose from to eat without having to grow it, or walk 30 miles for it. We are so blessed!"

"When your perception is based on your physical reality, it causes you to be limited. When your perception is based on spiritual or universal reality, then, you become free from current (physical) beliefs that hold you back, you become... LIMITLESS!"

"Everyone goes through hard times, what differs is your perception. Is it permanent or temporary? Almost all hard times are temporary; they just feel very permanent or "concrete" at the time. Energetically this is important! Shift your perspective to temporary, whatever it is, because then it becomes more fluid. When energy is fluid it can move in and out, however, concrete energy stays for much longer then it needs too!"

"Being in a relationship is a choice, you can leave at anytime. So behave like you are choosing to be there, not like you have nowhere better to go."

"Everyone wants to learn how to access their higher consciousness, they would like to be able to learn and expand their awareness by tapping into it. Did you know that you tap into it every night? Then, you block all of that amazing information as you awaken."

"Worry less, enjoy more, because more often then not, things will work out anyway..."

How To Use This Section of the Book:

"When working with the Universe its not about how fast you can tread water, it's about your technique. Imagine that the Universe is a big lake. Treading water faster then another does not get you better results, it just makes you more tired! If you understand the technique, you can relax, save your energy while achieving the same results!"

"True or false... I have no control over what happens to me in my life, it was predestined for me before I was born... FALSE!!!! Only some things are in your life plan, but the way you handle them is not. You have a tremendous amount of control over what happens in your lifetime and do not ever let anyone tell you otherwise!"

"Life is not complicated, your perspective is..."

"Life is about experiences. If you are afraid to test the water, you will never know what it is like to swim in the ocean, or better yet, with the dolphins!"

"What you see in someone else is usually only 10% of who they really are. See, your true identity exists beyond what your eyes can see, in other words, there is so much more to you then you often realize!"

"Alignment is spiritual, physical and mental, therefore, it is most important to make choices that are in alignment with who you want to be, or where you want to go in life. That creates a change in the scenery so to speak. If you make choices that are not in alignment with those things, don't be surprised at the view you do get. You are a reflection of the choices you make!"

"People do not like to admit when they might be part of their own problem, in fact, they become defensive about it. When you truly understand the role that you play in your own life. Especially when encountering a problem, you become a powerful component. Until then, you just become a victim to everyone else's behavior."

"Explore life to find your path, inevitably along this journey you will leave footprints. Because of this, it is important not to follow someone else's footprints to find your path, or you will be on their journey."

"People have been trained from a very young age to take the path of resistance, the path of nothing is easy, and life is hard. So it is the path most people look for, it is the path that your mind is most comfortable with. However, when you take a step back for a minute, more often than not, you will realize the path of least resistance is just two steps to the right..."

"Pick your battles, 95% of arguments are a waste of time and ego related. Do not waste this valuable energy. Imagine this, you don't leave your car running all of the time, even when you are at home watching TV. You don't leave all of the lights on in your house in the daytime, when you go to work. Why? Because, it is a waste of valuable energy! The energy used to operate your physical and spiritual system is precious, use it wisely not wastefully."

"Sometimes when things are not going the way that you want in life, it is time to scrap that plan and make a new one. Do not force yourself to stick with a plan that is not working, go back to the drawing board and create a better picture!"

"Happiness can be just as contagious as misery."

"Many times people find it very hard to break attachments! If something is not working after reasonable effort…LET IT GO! When you are focusing your energy towards something that is not manifesting, it is "stuck", or hung up somewhere. Letting things go can be exhilarating! On an energetic level you will feel a lot lighter, because the tension is then released!"

"You should continue to restructure your life's plan to fit your current desires throughout your lifetime. Imagine if you built a house when you were 7, you probably want different things in the house when you are 16, 35, 52 and so on. Does your life's blueprint fit your old wants or your current needs?"

"Distracting yourself from stress is common through TV, computer, drinking, etc. However, energetically those things can be time consuming and useless. It's like taking cold medicine when you are sick, then running around in a snowstorm with your coat off everyday. If you choose to do this, don't come home wondering why you are not feeling any better!"

"When you focus on managing the turmoil on the inside, it will naturally resolve the turmoil on the outside, not the other way around!"

"People should stop wasting energy trying to fix things that might not be broken, because many times they make the mistake of thinking something is broken, when it's really in a state of change. People do not break, things break, people are in a constant state of change and many times that's a good thing."

"If we lived in a world with no fear. Then you would never discover the courage you have within."

"Know there's more, because there is… Go after what you want, because you can… Live your dream life, because you're meant to… Don't settle, because everyone else does…"

Author Bio:

Spiritual teacher and best selling author Jennifer O'Neill is devoted to helping others learn how to live a happier life through her books, readings and workshops. The focus of her writing and teaching is to simplify the process of using the spiritual tools and gifts you were born with in a way that fits into your everyday life.

She is the author of several books including Soul DNA, Inspirational Quotes, Keys To The Spirit World, The Pursuit of Happiness, and several more to be released this year. Jennifer is also one of Hawaii's top psychics and the leading expert in the field of Soul DNA, as well as the originator of the Soul DNA© process. She has spent the last twenty years as a professional psychic and spiritual teacher helping people all over the world with their spiritual growth.

You can find information on Jennifer's radio show, blog, books and workshops on her website www.hawaiihealings.com.

Made in the USA
Lexington, KY
11 June 2014